Missionary Richard Browning

The Struggle for Meaning

W9-CVY-361

William Powell Tuck, Editor

Judson Press ® Valley Forge

THE STRUGGLE FOR MEANING
Copyright © 1977
Judson Press, Valley Forge, PA 19481

All rights reserved. No part of this publication may be reproduced, stored in a retrieval system, or transmitted in any form or by any means, electronic, mechanical, photocopying, or otherwise, without the prior permission of the copyright owner, except for brief quotations included in a review of the book.

Versions of the Bible quoted in this book are:

The Holy Bible, King James Version.

The Revised Standard Version of the Bible, copyrighted 1952 and 1971 by the Division of Christian Education of the National Council of the Churches of Christ in the United States of America. Used by permission.

Good News for Modern Man, The New Testament and Psalms in Today's English Version. Copyright © American Bible Society, 1966, 1970, 1971.

The New English Bible, Copyright © The Delegates of the Oxford University Press and The Syndics of the Cambridge University Press, 1961, 1970.

The New Testament in Modern English, rev. ed. Copyright © J. B. Phillips 1972. Used by permission of The Macmillan Company and Geoffrey Bles, Ltd.

The Bible: A New Translation by James Moffatt. Copyright 1954 by James Moffatt. Reprinted by permission of Harper & Row, Publishers, Inc.

Library of Congress Cataloging in Publication Data
Main entry under title:

The Struggle for meaning.

  Includes bibliographical references.
  1. Baptists—Sermons. 2. Sermons, American.
I. Tuck, William P.
BX6333.A1S77   252'.06   76-48747
ISBN 0-8170-0724-5

The name JUDSON PRESS is registered as a trademark in the U.S. Patent Office.
Printed in the U.S.A.

To Emily,
who has enriched
my life
with meaning

Contents

Preface

We do not have to put our ears to the ground to sense the discord and displacement within our society today. An alarm of disquietude has resounded within us. It is felt on global as well as on national levels. Voices, sounding like apocalyptic prophets, are screaming the certainty of doomsday. Giant problems have arisen because of the sharp rise in population, productivity, and pollution. Daily on our newsstands and over our television sets we are reminded of world hunger and disease, wars and revolutions, accidents and disasters, political and business corruption, government and industrial mismanagement, the crumbling inner cities and expanding suburbs, the loosening of family and sexual standards, moral and religious decline, uncontrolled inflation, poverty and unemployment, and the rising crime rate and power of organized crime. Demands for liberation have been asserted by blacks and other racial minorities, by women, and by underdeveloped countries. Although scientific and technological advances have enabled us to live more comfortably, more securely, and longer; many seem restless, bored, rebellious, frightened, and disturbed.

The titles alone of some of our contemporary literature reflect the dilemma of our present age: T. S. Eliot's *The Waste Land* and "The Hollow Men," Samuel Beckett's *Endgame,* William Faulkner's *Sound and Fury,* Jean-Paul Sartre's *No Exit,* Franz Kafka's *The Trial,* Albert Camus' *The Plague* and *The Stranger,* Arthur Miller's *After the Fall,* Graham Greene's *It's a Battlefield,* and most expressively Eugene O'Neill's *Long Day's Journey into Night.* Our sense of alienation, isolation, and the loss of any transcendent, divine dimension are vividly portrayed in the contemporary theater of the absurd by playwrights, such as Ionesco, Albee, Beckett, Arrabal, and others. In their plays they have touched the monsters within us and society and have exposed us to an existence which is depicted as being without dependable foundations, values, or direction. Are they correct? In much of our music, art, literature, drama, and even in some of modern theology, there is a pervading sense of meaningless- ness. *"Man can bear great physical or spiritual hardship,"* Elton Trueblood notes, *"but what he cannot bear is the sense of meaninglessness.* We must find some way in which our lives count, in which they seem important, or we go mad." [1]

In a world which many see as mad already, how can we keep our sanity? Do we merely live out our existence in "quiet desperation," or can we know that life is really worth living? Several centuries ago the Greek philosopher Socrates observed that the unexamined life is not worth living. Today we are being forced as never before to examine our reason for living. Although this self-examination may sound like a somber note, it can be the challenge to lift us out of a daily cycle of working, eating, and resting without reflecting on the meaning or purpose of anything we do. Can we continue to live day after day, year after year, without some goal or direction? The question of meaning sooner or later startles each of us with its penetrating inquiries: "Why am I alive?" "What does my life mean?" "Will it matter that I lived?" "Judging whether life is or is not worth living," noted Albert Camus, "amounts to answering the fundamental question of philosophy." [2] The question of meaning then becomes not merely an abstract philosophical enigma but a dilemma which confronts every man or woman. Charles Schulz, our "pop theologian" today, has illustrated the way some of us attempt to evade this struggle in a conversation between Charlie Brown and Lucy. As they are walking along, Lucy inquires, "You know what your trouble is, Charlie Brown? The whole trouble with you is you don't understand the meaning of life!" Turning toward her, Charlie Brown asks, "Do *you* understand the meaning of life?" "We're not talking about me," Lucy replies, "we're talking about you!" We might wish we could have it that way, but we cannot. The question about the meaning of life is individual and personal. Our inquiry cannot be satisfied with life in general but with my life and your life. "Is life worthwhile?" is essentially the question of each one of us. It is your question and mine.

How do we determine the meaning of our lives? Some have measured the meaningfulness of their lives by whether or not they are happy. But how do you measure happiness? As a modern jingle phrased it: "Happiness is different things to different people." Some people judge their happiness in terms of material possessions, or financial security, or sexual satisfaction, or power and prestige, or intellectual attainments. Can we be happy with "things" if we are unhappy with ourselves? In a real sense nothing external can have much meaning for us unless we have found reconciliation within our deepest self. The brokenness and distortion in the world cannot be disentangled until we have resolved the anxiety, rejection, and hostility toward ourselves. In *The New Being,* Paul Tillich proclaims that one finds the deepest kind of acceptance where one "accepts one's self as something which is eternally important, eternally loved, eternally accepted. The disgust at one's self, the hatred of one's self has disappeared. There is a center, a direction, a meaning for life."[3]

The sermons in this book are unapologetically rooted in the reality of the Christian faith. The ministers whose sermons are included in this volume declare in a variety of ways, as William James wrote in the article "Is Life Worth Living?", "that my final appeal is to nothing more recondite than religious faith."[4] This is a needed word for today and a word which gives direction and hope. Here is guidance from those who have struggled with the reality of this world and still proclaim the reality of the presence of God in the midst of their struggles. Meaning is not always the same for every life, nor always understood or followed. It is sometimes partially or even provisionally understood, but ultimately meaning for life is related to the God who was "in Christ reconciling the world to himself."

While visiting the city of Copenhagen, I was riding on a tour bus through the "hippie" area of the city. Painted graffito style on the side of a brick building were the words: "Fifty buses pass here a day. Tourist, who are you?" "Who am I?" I thought, as I reflected on that sign. Today I could define my life in terms of my vocation, but who would I be when I retire or if I lost my job? Who am I in terms of what I am? That is the real question for me and everyone. It is the personal question of my life's meaning. I cannot avoid answering it. It is the question of every person.

The contributors to this volume include pastors, theological professors, and denominational leaders who are actively involved in the ministry of the church. I appreciate their interest and participation in this book. I also want to thank Mrs. F. S. Paris for her diligent typing of the manuscript.

William Powell Tuck

The Search

Matthew 13:45-46

Kelly Miller Smith

The search is on.

The problem is that we are rarely able to identify the object of our search. We simply know that there must be more than this. Perhaps in a very general way we know that we are seeking for that elusive thing called meaning of life. We know that things ought to make some sort of sense—some rhyme or reason. But in a deeper and more profound sense we do not really know what we are looking for. This is quite evident in the way we conduct the search. We know there

---

Kelly Miller Smith, a Mississippi native, is pastor of the First Baptist Church, Capitol Hill, Nashville, Tennessee, and Assistant Dean, Vanderbilt University Divinity School. He is a graduate of Morehouse College and Howard University of Religion, Washington, D.C. He has done additional study at Vanderbilt and Harvard University. His many places of leadership include serving as President of the Nashville Branch, NAACP, 1956–1959; President, Tennessee Baptist Leadership Education Congress, 1965–1969; Southern Regional Council; and as a member of the Faith and Order Commission of the World Council of Churches. He has contributed articles and sermons to magazines and books, including *Best Black Sermons, The Pulpit Speaks on Race,* and *To Be a Person of Integrity. Ebony* magazine listed him as "One of America's Ten Most Outstanding Preachers," and in 1969 he was named "Clergyman of the Year" by Religious Heritage of America.

are missing pieces, but we are still trying to put round pegs in square holes.

We tend to identify that which seems to respond to our negative experiences as the objects of our search. So, the oppressed say that relief from oppression is all that is needed. Those whose cheeks have been bathed with the tears of sadness and who have had to drink too deeply from the cup of bitterness will say that the pearl of great price is rational happiness. It is relief from the tears which flow all too copiously. Those who know the meaning of poverty are likely to say that the pearl of great price, the thing for which they seek, their ultimate objective, is to find relief from the material poverty through material gain. There are those who know stress and strain, who know what it is to have their hearts bruised and battered and broken and their spirits enshrouded in mourning, who say that the pearl of great price is peace of mind—at any cost.

To be sure, these are needs and ought to be fulfilled. The Christian faith addresses these issues in a most meaningful way. The mistake too often made, however, is that of thinking that once these urgent matters are corrected, *all* needs are covered. Not so!

Then, there are those who have long since stopped trying to define the object of their search or even to admit that they are searching. They simply have found what they consider to be alternatives to it. They are the ones who cop out. They are the ones who find a level of living which is designed to blot out the hunger and thirst which is as yet unsatisfied. They are the ones who take drug trips, sometimes *religious* trips, in order to blot out the real thirst that is there. Sometimes our stained glass windows not only keep us from seeing what is inside the church building but also keep us from seeing what is inside ourselves and, more importantly, what is not inside ourselves. And so the search goes on.

What is the pearl of great price? What is the elusive thing that fills the emptiness, that elusive piece of the puzzle of life which will help us to find something called meaning? As is so characteristic of Jesus, he addresses himself very candidly and forthrightly to this issue. He says that the pearl of great price is something called the kingdom of heaven. This, of course, does not mean eating pie in the sky when you die by and by. The reference is to a quality of life and the acceptance of the sovereignty of God. If there is anything that we should reach out for now, it is for the sovereignty of God, because circumstances of chaos remind us of our need for a sovereign. When the computer doesn't seem to compute, when the answers seem not to come and we look in the back of the book and the answers are not there, when it seems that the cause and effect relationship has broken down, then we have chaos on our hands, and chaos reminds us that we need to say, "Lead me to the rock that is higher than I."

The kingdom of heaven refers to the sovereignty of God, the acceptance of the rulership of God. That is the umbrella under which our lives ought to be lived. There is another picture of the kingdom of heaven or of the acceptance of the sovereignty of God: a man found a treasure in a field. When he found it, he recognized that it was worth more than all else which he owned; so he sold everything to buy the field and get the treasure. There is the message: search until you find meaning, substance, essence, and when you find it, bet everything you have on it.

There are some prerequisites to finding the pearl of great price, the ultimate object of our search. There are some ways in which we look for it which will never yield the pearl. For one thing, there must be a recognition of the importance of the internal, as well as the external. That says a great deal in our society. We assign values on the basis of that which meets the eye, that which impresses outwardly, that which is external in one way or the other, that which impresses others. We assign values in terms of external success. But there is no greater need which our society has than the building of inner resources; than the recognition of the fact that people have hungers which bread alone cannot satisfy; that they have needs which things cannot satisfy. Much of what happens that is evil in our society is due not to what happens externally, but to what either happens or fails to happen internally.

We are told that, as humans, we look on the outward appearance, but God looks on the heart. Jesus says, "What is a man profited if he shall gain the whole world and lose his inner self?"

The story has been told of a man who went to a watch repairman with only the two hands of his watch. When he placed these hands on the counter, he told the repairman, "Fix 'em." The watch repairman asked him for the rest of the watch, but he explained, "Why, the rest of the watch is at home. But that part is all right. It is just these hands that won't keep time." Of course, the repairman told him something which all who would have life whisper its meaning to them should hear: "But it must be corrected on the inside in order for the hands on the outside to work properly." Ridiculous? Not at all. This is as logical as some of our approaches to problems and issues of our day. It is as logical as the enlargement of police forces to deal with the problems and frustrations of members of the human family which manifest themselves in deviant behavior. It is as logical as spending the greater part of our national budget to increase our ability to kill and maim as the chief instrument of international polity. "But it must be corrected on the inside in order for the hands to work properly on the outside." The object of our search will not be realized until and unless we give major attention to our inner selves, our inner hungers, our inner thirsts, and our inner needs.

Secondly, the prerequisite for finding the pearl of great price, that is, the giving of ourselves over to the sovereignty of God, is to discover the shallowness, the meaninglessness of the kind of instrumentalism which so characterizes our age. This utilitarianism—the belief that the only thing that is of value is that which serves a particular useful purpose for me—motivates our choice of a marital partner, governs the courses which students take in schools (so that a student who is going to be an engineer, for example, sees no need to study Shakespeare or to study music or to become acquainted with the black experience, for he does not see how this will be useful in the pursuit of his career in engineering), and is tragically true in religion.

Many have joined the "peace of mind cult" and have come to believe that the purpose of religion is for us to obtain for ourselves something called peace of mind, which is sub-Christian and pagan. It is selfish to go to church to receive peace of mind. The kingdom, then, becomes a glorified aspirin tablet, a tranquilizer. This is utilitarianism, too. This is failing to recognize the fact, the most important fact, that God has created us for himself, and we shall know restlessness, we shall know anxiety, until we rest with him. This is unchanged. Jesus tells us, "Seek ye first not peace of mind. Seek ye first not the things which can instrumentally be brought to you through the trappings of the experiences of religion. Seek ye first the kingdom of heaven, the sovereignty of God, the acknowledgment of a rulership of God. Seek this first, and all of these other things shall be added unto you." So peace of mind comes—but not by our seeking it. Find the pearl of great price. Allow God to be the ruling force in your life. You will discover that in that very process something happens which satisfies the other needs which we have.

One thing that is very evident in both of the parables is the fact of the willingness to invest something, to give up something in the interest of that which is of supreme value. I suspect that this is also one of our great problems—the unwillingness to be cut loose from something, to give up something in the interest of this pursuit. The man who was plowing in the field sold all that he had so that he could buy the field and then own the treasure that was buried there. The merchant gathered up all of his other jewels and got rid of them, cut himself loose from them, because the pearl which he had been seeking was of greater value.

There are some things from which we are not willing to extricate ourselves. Some things are a little too precious to us. These may be material things, but more often than not they are other kinds of things. Sometimes they are our attitudes, which we will not change. Sometimes it is an unwillingness to get out of the way. This may be an important investment—for you simply to get out of somebody's way. It can be an unwillingness to change attitudes which will change the whole posture and image of the Christian church. Is it not tragic that all too often those who can call the name of Jesus Christ in the most pious tones are also those who might correctly be characterized as the bishops of bigotry and the prophets of prejudice? Is it not tragic that the church, in human eyes, has become the custodian of the status quo? Is it not tragically true, as Martin Luther King once put it, that if the church is a light at all, it is a taillight rather than a headlight? Is it not tragically true that when the nations have been needing a prophetic voice, they have received from the church a pathetic echo?

Perhaps we have not put aside enough of the extraneous. These are attitudes and dispositions from which we must cut ourselves loose if we are seriously in quest of the pearl of great price. Take another look at this picture of the kingdom of heaven, the sovereignty of God. A merchant seeking to find pearls found one of special value; so he went and sold everything he had and bought it.

Consciously or unconsciously, we are in search of something. If we find it by finding the kingdom of God—the pearl of great price—life will whisper its meaning unto our souls. And then we shall be priests and prophets, and we shall lead others in life's creative search.

A Strategy
for Survival

John 15:12-13; 1 Corinthians 11:23-24

John Killinger

We have passed, we are told, from the age of plenty into the era
of survival.

That is a generalization, of course. Some people have never had
plenty. There are at this very moment, in some nation where the sun is
not shining, children whose sleep is broken by the pains of hunger.
Their stomachs are ulcerated from lack of food.

But most of us have had more than enough, discounting our
greed, and now the sound of the warning is ominous.

John Killinger, writer and lecturer, is professor of Preaching,
Worship, and Literature at the Divinity School of Vanderbilt
University in Nashville, Tennessee. A graduate of Baylor
University, the University of Kentucky, M.A. and Ph. D., Harvard
University, S.T.B., and Princeton Theological Seminary, Th.D.,
he has taught at Georgetown College, Princeton Seminary, the
University of Chicago, and was academic dean of Kentucky
Southern College before moving to Nashville in 1965. He served
as theologian in residence at the American Church in Paris,
France, for a year. A prolific writer, his more than seventeen
books include *Leave It to the Spirit, The Second Coming of the
Church, The Salvation Tree, The Fragile Presence: Transcendence in Modern Literature, Bread for the Wilderness—Wine for
the Journey,* and *The Eleven O'clock News and Other Experi-
mental Sermons.*

Survival. It is an ugly word. A threatening word. A frightening word. It conjures up pictures of us fighting, struggling, competing among ourselves for the world's remaining foodstuffs and raw materials. Not nation against nation and class against class—it has always been that way. But family against family, and soul against soul.

That is what scares us. To be turned into beasts again, just when we thought we were on the edge of the Great Society! To claw and scratch and kill—in order to live!

I find myself haunted of late by those first few scenes from the movie *2001,* where the first—or the last—bipeds fight with each other in little bands for control of an animal carcass or a waterhole.

How far have we really come from that?

Maybe there is a parable of how far we have come in Piers Paul Read's recent book, *Alive: The Story of the Andes Survivors.* It is a remarkable story—a true story—of forty-five persons who crashed in the rugged, snowcrested mountains of South America and of the sixteen of them who lived more than two months through that incredible ordeal to return to their homes and families.

The odds were strongly against survival. Of the thirty-two persons still alive after the plane crash, many were injured. One had a steel tube thrust into his stomach. Another's calf was twisted around over his shin, leaving his leg bone completely exposed. Others had broken limbs, head injuries, internal pains. They had little food—some dates, plums, crackers, a few candy bars, a little jelly, and some wine. Their clothing was totally inadequate for the subfreezing temperatures. The plane had been ripped in two by the impact of the crash, and the biting winds howled through the fuselage.

Yet sixteen of the thirty-two survivors lived for seventy days under those extreme circumstances.

How did they do it?

The miracle is no secret. It had to do with how they cared for each other. The well tended the hurt. Even the boy with a steel pipe in his stomach worked untiringly to help those who were hurt worse than he. They slept huddled in each other's arms to share their warmth. They voluntarily rationed their food, a square of chocolate a day and small cup of wine drunk from a cap of a deodorant can.

And they prayed—as most of them had never prayed before.

Survival of the fittest? Theodore Dreiser, the novelist, must have seen something as a child which he never forgot and which he put in a novel as the truest picture of life as he knew it. It was a classic struggle between a lobster and a squid in a fish tank outside a grocery store. Every day the small boy would come down to the store to check the progress of the battle. Each day another piece of the squid's tentacles would be missing. Gradually the lobster was wearing the squid down. For a while, the squid emitted a murky substance in the water and escaped through it. But finally hunger and the battle took their toll, and the squid could no longer do its trick. One day it was simply too battered and spent to move. The lobster reached out one deliberate claw and it was over. Just like that.

"You'd better be prepared," Dreiser was saying. "Life is like that. When the chips are down, don't count on anyone. We are all enemies in the struggle to survive. We will kill to live." [1]

But it wasn't that way with the people on the mountain. "It was something no one could have imagined," one man afterwards told a priest. "I used to go to mass every Sunday, and Holy Communion had become something automatic. But up there, seeing so many miracles, being so near God, almost touching Him, I learned otherwise. Now I pray to God to give me strength and stop me slipping back to what I used to be. I have learned that life is love, and that love is giving to your neighbor. The soul of a man is the best thing about him. There is nothing better than giving to a fellow human being. . . ." [2]

Imagine! Nothing better than giving to a fellow human being! Even when there seemed to be so little to give.

I hear echoes of Paul in that: "I will show you a better way—the best way," he said. And then he began the thirteenth chapter of First Corinthians, the song of love and how it endures beyond everything else.

The man went to Communion every Sunday, and it was automatic. But the experience of the mountain—of being without, of nearly starving, or freezing—had really shown him what Communion was all about. It was about caring for others and laying down one's life for his friends.

What was it Luther said about the church? It is where the Word of God is preached and the sacraments are rightly administered. Yes and no. That is part of it.

But maybe we can improve on what Luther said.

The church is where we learn what life is about, and it is where we learn to care and be cared for.

The church is the center of care. And if it isn't—why, then, we haven't understood the meaning of Jesus' teachings and his death at all, and we aren't the church. We are only pretending to be the church. Church is where people care.

"How do you teach somebody to care?" a young man recently asked his teacher.

The teacher thought a moment, and then he said, "First, I guess you have to experience care, to know that you yourself are cared for; and then you can care for others."

That is true, isn't it? First we must learn that we are cared for. And that, in turn, releases something in us, frees us to care for others. And this *process* is what church is about. Not the preservation of dogma and doctrine. Not the funding of an organization or the erecting of a steeple. But the experience of care. Knowing the love of God through one another.

We were down under recently, my wife and I, overcome with caring. And in the midst of it we were deluged by relatives, some of whom seemed not to care. Resentment was easy. "Don't they care about anybody but themselves?" we asked.

And then a woman of the congregation with whom we worship did a beautiful thing. She showed up at our door with a basketful of homemade muffins and a large container of tea. "I thought it would make things easier," she said. And from somewhere, through her gift of caring, came the strength we needed to care in return. Every time we ate a muffin or tasted the tea, I thought of Communion—the bread and the wine. And it lifted my heart.

"Lift up your hearts."

"We lift them unto the Lord!"

There is one more thing I didn't tell you about how those people on the frozen mountain survived.

They became cannibals.

One day it dawned on them that there was no other way. The food was gone. Their strength was waning. If they were to survive, they must overcome one of the deepest of human taboos and eat the flesh of those who had died, still perfectly preserved in the snow and ice.

It was a repugnant idea. They did not think they could do it. They did not think they *should* do it—at first.

They argued about doing it. Finally one man said, "What do you think *they* would have thought? . . . I know that if my dead body could help you to stay alive, then I'd certainly want you to use it."[3]

It was a forceful argument: they knew they would wish the same.

At last, four men went out into the snow and uncovered a body. One of them knelt and bared the skin of the body. In deepest silence, he cut into the flesh with a piece of broken glass.

The body was frozen and difficult to cut. But at last twenty small pieces of flesh had been sliced away. They were laid on the plane's roof to dry in the sun.

The man who had done the cutting saw that he must be first. He prayed that God would help him to do what he felt was right. Then he took a piece of flesh in his hand. He hesitated. For a moment he seemed paralyzed. Then he put the flesh in his mouth and swallowed.

For two months they stayed alive on human flesh. Eventually it provided sufficient strength for two of their number to hike through the waist-deep snow over treacherous mountainsides and deliver the message that fourteen of their friends were still alive at the summit.

When they were all rescued and the word had got out that they had survived by eating the bodies of their friends, many people were shocked and outraged. At a press conference, the room was deathly quiet as their spokesman told why they did it.

"We thought to ourselves that if Jesus at His last supper had shared His flesh and blood with His apostles," he said, "then it was a sign to us that we should do the same—take the flesh and blood as an intimate communion between us all."[4]

"This is my body, which is for you . . ."—an intimate communion between us all.

We are back to the lobster and the squid, aren't we? We *do* survive by feeding on others. Only there is a difference. "Love one another as I have loved you." We have known love and care. We have fed on Christ and on one another. Therefore we offer ourselves as food to others. We live to die, and have in order to give.

It makes everything so much easier and clearer.

Shortages? We shall always have enough to share, so long as we have anything at all. World hunger? We managed to send men to the moon; we can find ways of feeding and clothing the multitudes. Justice for everyone? The Christian demands it. The donation of organs at the time of death? How can we do less?

"Don't you know," said the apostle, "you are not your own? You are bought with a price." Slave language—from a time of slave culture.

But does that bother us? Who wouldn't willingly serve as his slave?

Church is where we learn to care and be cared for.

Prayer. Deliver us, Father, from not caring into being generous with ourselves and everything we have. Let grace run down like the mountain streams. Let the earth be renewed and filled with our joy. Through Jesus, our Lord of the cross. Amen.

The True Believer

John 9:35-38; Mark 9:20-24

Carlyle Marney

Across forty years of inquiry I should like to have been *a true believer*, I think. In three chapters, the Koran makes this an attractive proposition, especially when compared to the fate of the unbeliever. Thomas Carlyle's "Peasant Saint" is a true believer. In my years of ministry I have known one true believer, a peasant saint in Paraguay, and I think I knew another one in the White Mountains of Arizona, but that is all.

In early English literature, Piers Plow-man is Christ walking the

---

Carlyle Marney is Director of the Interpreter's House, Lake Junaluska, North Carolina. Formerly he was pastor of the Myers Park Baptist Church, Charlotte, North Carolina, and First Baptist Church, Austin, Texas. In 1972 he was appointed Visiting Professor at Duke Divinity School. He is a graduate of Carson-Newman College and received his Th.M. and Th.D. degrees from the Southern Baptist Theological Seminary. He has served as trustee for the *Christian Century,* a member of the board of *Theology Today, Religion in Life,* editor of the Religious Book Club, and Vice-President-at-Large of the National Council of Churches. He was named to *Who's Who in America* in 1965. He is the author of twelve books, which include *Structures of Prejudice, The Recovery of the Person, He Became Like Us, The Coming Faith,* and *Priests to Each Other.* Wake Forest University honored him with a Lit.D. degree, and Johnson C. Smith University with a D.D.

English fields bearing that plain answer to life's riddles which the institutional church had already forgotten how to give seven hundred years ago. Yet, not even since Piers Plow-man has the church quit its dying, though it never really does die. Nor for the last seven hundred years has it been possible for one *who knows the world at all* to be a true believer. Yet, I should like to have been a true believer, I think.

But now, and especially for the last 140 years, there have been implications in being a true believer for which I have great distaste. There are demands by which I cannot qualify. The definition of a true believer would make me appear an infidel compared to the truly true believer. Petty implications require a life of loyal acceptance of all that is said in the name of religion by my local expert. This means a life of loyalty to a set of unexamined concepts, received from unquestioned oracles, who are ordained by bishops to tell me these things. It requires the unquestioned adoption of a special lingo of pious intimacy with the Eternal, which assumes that I have a special relation with the Eternal, which I presume you not to have. It requires you to talk the lingo that I am wishing to use if we are to belong to each other.

To be a true believer implies that I will not question any details of the biblical revolution or revelation even when I am in second year high school biology. It means that I must have abandoned all modern knowledge and discoveries except those views which support my premises. I must have all answers and no questions; I must sport an unblemished record of believing; I must preach always as if I had no doubts. I must avoid the very climate of independent thinking and express this stance in a totalitarian support of the establishment, its pattern, its institutions, and its dogmas.

Now the only trouble I have with this definition of the true believer is that it seems to require the destruction of humanity as well as God. It requires me to be stupid; it requires me to be naive; it requires of me a pride-filled exclusivism, blindness, ignorance, hypocrisy, and conformism. It dehumanizes me in a kind of spiritual mesmerization; but worse, this kind of stupid faith eliminates so many grand rascals that I want to keep.

In my private bible, *The Human Situation,* MacNeile Dixon, the Gifford lecturer of thirty years ago, says something like this:

> How sad are the virtuous, how cheerful and light-hearted so often the profane. How gay and gallant, how amusing so many of the rascals! My affections have, I suppose, betrayed or undermined my moral principles.

Holiness is a strong perfume, and a little of it goes a long way in the world. I have never been very clear whether it was compatible with laughter, and I should be very loath to bid an eternal farewell to laughter.[1]

How choleric the believer's believer!

Also, the demands of being a true believer plow up too many of the heretics from whom I have learned. I should have to give up that George Bernard Shaw who gave me the book of Genesis again; I should even have to bid farewell to Julian Huxley who gave me biology, that Bertrand Russell of my youth, and that gorgeous poet, Nietzsche, of *Beyond Good and Evil*. What would we do without these in our youth? And Feuerbach, too, his vibrant negative theology, so close to an utter negation of theism. This kind of faith also presupposes grossness and immorality in persons who may be more saintly than the fair believer upon whom their soilure might rub off. This kind of true belief puts me in the company of the dull; it makes me live a life that has known only the death of verve, creativity, and imagination. It has lost the fire of its drama, the agony of discontent, the flame of its passion, and the contradiction of its despair.

I have met, for twenty-eight years, such miserable people around the churches. They huddle up in clusters just inside the doors like crickets on a change-of-the-weather day. There is too often among us, I find, no real requirement for goodness, no genuine demand for integrity, no open concern for anything. The church has become a magnificent place to hide. Whoever goes to church to be who he is or she is? You go to church to be who-you-hope-to-God-you-look-like-you-are! Who could endure coming to church to be who you are?

So, all my life, I have been seeking another way to be a true believer. A way that does not avoid the obvious. A way to believe that does not distort the personal. A way to believe that does not deny my own cleavages and despairs. A way to believe that does not claim the impossible or shellac the unbelievable. A way to believe that does not eliminate the seeker-saint and the doubter-saint and the hungry-saint and the sinner-saint. There must be another way to be a true believer. There must be another kind.

As a matter of fact, there is. "Lord, I believe," one said, "and he worshiped him." There is another passage, "Lord, I believe; help Thou mine unbelief."

In the boyhood of Karl Barth stands the shadowy influence of an obscure reformed theologian, Kohlbrugge, called "the outsider." One day he ran head-on into a group of excited pietists who pinned him to the corner by saying, "Dr. Kohlbrugge, have you met the Lord?" The old half-free-thinker said finally, "Yah." And they said, "Where have you met the Lord?" And he said, "On Golgotha."

There are depths of belief in many a half-believer more redemptive than any professional can claim. What living person can boast an unblemished record of believing?

Look, then, *at faith as half-believing.* Now it doesn't take all the sense in the world to be a pastor. It requires just a little sense, a lot of smart, a lot of human openness, and a lot of waiting. As a boy, I needed a pastor ten years before he appeared, that fellow who could lean back against the small-town drugstore counter and hear out my unbelieving without being shocked. He was not much of a theologian, I guess, but he was a good man. He knew about doubt and disbelief and unbelief and rebellion. There was a pupil of the famous William James just three doors down the street, but his doubts had been so misread that he never talked to us anyway. He was the village infidel. He might have helped us; he could have helped us to see what a friend to faith doubt may be.

The best Christian life I have ever known confessed to me in his seventy-fourth year that his journey had been riddled with doubt. Who can grow to anything like maturity in this "godlessness of the night," so different from that "godlessness of the day" in which I grew up? Who can grow to anything like maturity in this "theatre of the absurd," where so many affairs are the absolute end? Who can go through it without being eaten up with negation and doubt?

When the self-revelation of God began to spill over Christ's most trusted disciples, they could hardly take it in. Transfiguration was a glory they had no notion how to describe, or keep. Everyone who mattered was there. They now discovered that when the Lord was in his glory, the only human beings who were even fit to confer with him were Moses and Elijah! Peter, carried away, said, "Lord, we never heard anything like this. Let's build three tabernacles." They had a built-in surety now. The old fears and reservations seemed like lies; doubts were gone; now they knew. Had they not seen that only Moses and Elijah could hold a candle to Him? "He has everything," they said. No more doubts; no more waiting. Everything was clearly settled. Now they could see their way through anything. No more doubts or risk; they had seen the transfiguration. If they could keep it forever! "Let's stay here forever," they said. "Let's keep this. Let's build three tabernacles to remember the day we had no doubt."

And then the terrible discovery. They went down the hill and walked in on the throes of an epileptic seizure. They felt themselves confronted with the ultimate of their inability to do or be anything. Faith was no longer so sure. And the disciples had to learn the hard way—in what agony I have learned—that faith is half-believing memory. Not much security lives in faith; no security from a previous experience can cancel out the risk. A person has to keep believing. The salt can lose its savor. Every day one has to be born again. There is no built-in guarantee that carries over from a previous victory. Yesterday's faith will not necessarily support today's threats; the most transcendent certainty is not transferable from me to you. The healing power and the failure are wrapped up in each moment of crisis, and faith is always a half-believing memory; everywhere *faith involves the memory of a meeting, some encounter.*

In the Scripture story we saw a man who believed so clearly he could move immediately into the sanctuary with us for worship; and, we saw, on the other hand, a man so caught in the contradictions that he could only confess his recurrent unbelief. But, he put a hyphen where it belonged: between I-Thou, cross-resurrection, you-me, belief-unbelief, and the tie cannot be separated. The movement is always from the meeting to worship or from the meeting to believing-unbelief. I think we have been mistaken when we thought faith ever required unblemished believing.

Faith. Define faith? Faith is simply your inability-to-walk-away-from. Faith is to-be-unable-utterly-to-abandon. Faith is to be unable to live as if a meeting or a memory were not back there. Faith is to be unable to abandon some high relationship that still has long arms to reach me out of my long-gone adolescence—some moment when I met the Eternal or the Beyond, or the Holy, or the Great Mystery, or the Other, or the Brother, or the Father, or the Sister, or the One. So this faith lives with and breeds despair, loneliness, and grief, and even an interim secularism as we see with many modern Jews, but it certainly does not breed blind misjudgment of our situation. The true believer is one unable to abandon one's memories of some meeting with a Thou. Sometime we may but vaguely remember the meeting, but it has long arms to reach for us in some far place of adulthood and bring us back.

I remember him, that beautiful French-Italian-New Englander who came to the university with 253 hours of philosophy and no bachelor's degree. He had been for twenty years a Passionist teacher; but now excommunicated, he had gone counter to his cult, his culture, and God. Abandoned by his family, buffeted by experts, he used to sit on the second row left, and his eyes always listened and spoke back, clinging to some meeting that he had known. One day he stopped to play in the sandbox with his three-year-old Debbie on his way out to the study. As he rose, brushing off the sand, to go back to his writing, Debbie, seized by the wonder of the relationship she had had with her father, said, "Daddy, let's do this three days." He came running into my neighboring study saying, "I've come to talk about transfiguration!" And the memory of some meeting I did not know flooded over him and me. This is a *faith,* when it can reach up from behind and grasp you so that you are unable utterly to abandon the way.

Faith is more. It is action! "The whole defense of religious faith hinges upon action," says William James. He is followed by Paul Lehmann and a holy company. ". . . this command that we shall put a stopper on our heart . . . and wait . . . [until somebody proves God]. This command, I say, to wait," says James, "seems to me the queerest idol ever manufactured in the philosophic cave." [2] Indeed we may wait to commit ourselves if we will, but if we do, we do so at our peril as much as if we believe. In either case we have acted believing or disbelieving, taking our lives in our hands. So what is action? *The action is interpretation.*

Faith in action is the way I live through which I interpret the things that come to me. Essentially such faith *is the interpretation that our highest values are really values, that they do count in the whole pattern of things, that the things for which we have worked are not simply our shallow dreams, that the meaning of the universe includes us.* What our hearts have longed for is answered by someone; our poor projections are exceeded only by that grace which we do meet and receive in some connection, so that in all our ways we interpret life as a sphere in which God has to do with us and we with God and there is no place to go where we can get away. This concrete active interpretation of life brings *requirements, discipline, mercies, joys, rebukes,* and I have discovered—even on the north end of lonely Wolf Pen Mountain, where I have been living a kind of intellectual exile for these last years—it brings also a very great joy. It is for this fundamental conviction that every sincere doubter is really struggling. It is out of this conviction that the whole rich process of religious belief grows, says Donald Baillie—the conviction that our ideals of love and duty have at their heart the very purpose and will of the universe and are laid down on us by one through whom, somehow, they are perfectly realized.

Some days, for the moment at least, I can do this. And when I can, I am in church. Sometimes it is on horseback in the Smokies with one of my daughters or some old wrangler friend of mine or some heathen. Sometimes it is just Elizabeth and me. Sometimes it is when the kids are home. Sometimes it is when they are away. Once in awhile it is when I am in a church service. It is almost never when I am preaching, because I have heard it before. Wherever it comes, that conviction that my life and my duty and my values and my love matter because the Eternal has cleansed them, I am in church, for the moment at least, knowing all the while that church will be out very soon.

So faith is another thing. It is action. It is worship and work. Lord, I believe, the man said, and he worshiped. It is the catalytic experience of the person. I remember him. I do not abandon him. I have interpreted him in my work and in my worship. Sometimes I worship, I say, and the option is alive.

During the Fondren Lectures at Southern Methodist University, I confessed that if I had a better doctrine of resurrection, I would be able to believe more steadily, but there were days when I didn't believe it at all. That grand theologian, Albert Outler, stopped me in the hall and said, "You shouldn't have said that." I said, "You're so smart, what should I have said, Albert?" He asked, "Whoever told you you had to believe every day?" I said, "Tell me, dear friend, when do I have to believe the resurrection?" And he said, to my unending appreciation, "The day you die and the day you have to die with somebody, you believe the resurrection of the dead!" Here I could say, "Yes," for in this situation I have been able always to say, "Lord, I believe," knowing all the while that in a few minutes church might be out for me, but I cling to the meeting with this Thou and crave its constant repetition.

"Lord, I believe, and he worshiped him." "Lord, I believe. Help Thou mine unbelief." It is a living option. Accept it or do without it and this is not an arrogance. It is a truth of Pascal's for, my friend, you either believe, or you deny, or you wonder about it all the time.

The "Foolish" Things Jesus Did

Matthew 21:18-22; John 2:1-11

Wesley Shrader

Critics of the New Testament charge that Jesus, during his lifetime, did and said many foolish things. At least three stories in the New Testament are examples of his unseemly behavior. The *first* concerns the story of his cursing the fig tree. He passed by and saw that the tree was barren. In anger he cursed it—never again would the tree bear fruit. But the Scriptures tell us it was not the season for ripe fruit! How could Jesus be angry with the tree when its time had not come? The *second* is the story of Jesus instructing his disciples to

---

Wesley Shrader, a native of Kentucky, is pastor of the Madison Avenue Baptist Church in New York City. He was educated at Western Kentucky State College and the Southern Baptist Theological Seminary in Louisville, Kentucky. He has done additional study at Columbia, Union Seminary, and Oxford. He has pastored churches in Kentucky, Virginia, North Carolina, and Pennsylvania, and served for three years as Associate Professor of Pastoral Theology at Yale University. He has served as a member of the Virginia Baptist Board of Missions and Education, Chairman of the Virginia Baptist Board's Executive Committee, and board of trustees, American Baptist Churches of Metropolitan New York. Feature articles by him have appeared in *Life, Reader's Digest, Esquire,* and others. Included among his eight books are *Forty Days Till Dawn, Anguished Men of God, Yeshua's Diary,* and *College Ruined Our Daughter.* Georgetown College has conferred an honorary D.D. upon him.

proceed to the lake and find a certain fish. In the fish's mouth there would be sufficient money for him to pay his temple taxes. Other people had to pay their taxes out of hard-earned money. Was this any way for a teacher in Galilee to behave? The *third* is the story of his turning the water into wine at the wedding festival in Cana. A great wedding feast was being held which lasted many days, usually seven or fourteen. The guests drank all the wine, and, of course, the host was embarrassed. Jesus turned the plain water of Cana into the best tasting wine at the festival—so much so that some of the guests said to the host, "You have saved the best wine to the very last." Now for the question which the critics ask, "Is this any way for a prophet or a teacher to use divine power—to turn water into wine?" Healing the palsied, yes; opening the eyes of the blind, yes; cleansing the leper, yes; feeding the hungry multitudes, yes—but not turning water into wine!

The concern of some of us in the contemporary church is not with answering critics who quarrel and quibble over biblical criticism, but our concern is with people who have embraced the Christian faith and who quietly and uncomfortably feel that Jesus was wrong in his *major* emphases. To these people his views are not only "foolish" but dangerous. He is accepted as the one who can get us from earth to heaven, but his major concerns are rejected; and they are rejected not only by professional critics of the Bible but also by many of our "best" Christian people. There are a number of examples which illustrate this point. I list four.

Jesus appeared to have a disdain for money and the things money could buy. He discovered the joys of the simple life and recommended that his followers "go thou and do likewise." He constantly warned about the perils of riches. He indicated that it would be difficult for a rich man to get into heaven, as difficult as for a camel to go through the eye' of a needle. He told the story of a successful man who filled his barns to overflowing, who tore down his barns in order to build bigger ones. He was a man who had gotten ahead, but Jesus said of him, "Thou fool, this night thy soul shall be required of thee." Yet, in spite of these warnings, we must confess that we have a tendency to measure success in terms of accumulated wealth. Often the *primary* reason for our existence seems to be to make money, save and hoard money, and spend money. The quiet, simple life, embracing Jesus' set of values, is not for us. Is he really foolish in his de-emphasis upon the pursuit of riches? Let a distraught, hectic, divided, insecure, and fearful society, which has made money its goal, answer that question.

The *second* point in Jesus' life, with which we have difficulty in identifying, is his insistence on challenging the power structures of the day. We admire him, but sometimes wonder why he deliberately agitated both political and ecclesiastical centers of power. We prefer living our lives in the midst of quiet desperation. We do not desire *noise, trouble, threats, divisions, controversy.* We *do* very much desire *peace, tranquillity,* and *quietude.* How nice it would have been if the disciples could have remained on the mount of transfiguration with Jesus, surrounded by peace, quiet, and beauty! But he insisted that they could not so remain. Into the world with its risks, dangers, and controversies they must go. This insistence cost him his life.

Why did he challenge the established power centers of his day? Exhibitionism? A name for himself? No, these centers of power were denying to his brothers and sisters, the children of God, the good things of life, including equal status under law and under God, as well as freedom. To be human, persons must have opportunity and freedom. Anything less dehumanizes them. Political and ecclesiastical power centers combined to prevent the achievement of dignity and selfhood. So, Jesus challenged them. Some of us fearfully and quietly ask, "Was he not foolish so to do?"

The *third* point of resistance among his friends is his rejection of violence as the way of achieving and maintaining the good life. Those in our country, who now control with power the nation's destiny as well as world events, know how we came by that power and how our privileged position is maintained. We came by it by brute violence, and we maintain it by brute violence. Furthermore, if our interests appear to be threatened by an uprising ninety miles away or six thousand miles from our shores, we have the capability and the will to make ourselves felt in a forceful and violent manner. When this occurs, Jesus' idea of "turning the cheek" and "walking the second mile" appears to be nonsense. We reach for the sword (jets and rockets) and swing at the enemy's head, not just his ear. In other words, though we love Jesus, we act as if he were impractical and hopelessly idealistic. His words, "Put up your sword; those who take the sword shall perish by the sword," sound strange in our ears. Yet, with the standoff in nuclear energy now achieved by world powers, with the massive possibilities of overkill, we must sometimes wonder if violence and force are the better way.

The *fourth* point of resistance is when Jesus says that his disciples must love each other and they must forgive their enemies! How can you love someone who has injured you? How can you forgive someone who does not deserve forgiveness? Sigmund Freud, in *Civilization and Its Discontents,* says it is impossible and unthinkable to love one's neighbor as one's self. He writes:

> The clue may be supplied by one of the ideal demands, as we have called them, of civilized society. It runs: "Thou shalt love thy neighbor as thyself." It is known throughout the world and is undoubtedly older than Christianity, which puts it forward as its proudest claim. Yet it is certainly not very old; even in historical times it was still strange to mankind. Let us adopt a naïve attitude towards it, as though we were hearing it for the first time; we shall be unable then to suppress a feeling of surprise and bewilderment. Why should we do it? What good will it do us? But, above all, how shall we achieve it? How can it be possible? My love is something valuable to me which I ought not to throw away without reflection. It imposes duties on me for whose fulfillment I must be ready to make sacrifices. If I love someone, he must deserve it in some way. . . . He deserves it if he is so like me in important ways that I can love myself in him; and he deserves it if he is so much more perfect than myself that I can love my ideal of my own self in him. Again, I have to love him if he is my friend's son, since the pain my friend would feel if any harm came to him would be my pain too—I should have to share it. But if he is a stranger to me and if he cannot attract me by any worth of his own or any significance that he may already have acquired for my emotional life, it will be hard for me to love him.[1]

In the same vein of thought the great writer Heine confesses:

> Mine is a most peaceable disposition. My wishes are: a humble cottage with a thatched roof, but a good bed, good food, the freshest milk and butter, flowers before my window, and a few fine trees before my door; and if God wants to make my happiness complete, he will grant me the joy of seeing some six or seven of my enemies hanging from those trees. Before their death I shall, moved in my heart, forgive them all the wrong they did me in their lifetime. One must, it is true, forgive one's enemies—but not before they have been hanged.[2]

These writings by non-Christian thinkers send a chill through my heart—not because I admire them, but because I sense that when the chips are down and the crisis is full-blown, we trust them more than we trust Jesus.

So in our day there is an abundance of uncertainty and confusion and listlessness. Moral values as accepted by Jesus are held halfheartedly, while the value structure of a secular world provides guidelines for our way of life. Political corruption, spiritual degeneration, and church apathy beset us. We have become split personalities torn by our timid commitment to Jesus and our unqualified commitment to a world whose ways and values are in direct opposition to those of our Lord.

Is there any balm in Gilead? Is there any hope that we shall breathe again the fresh air of his presence? There are several things which with haste must be done. First, there is the recognition of our plight as religious schizophrenics—loving Jesus but obeying the demands of the world. Second, it is best that we begin by examining our own lives and not that of our neighbor. Third, repentance can save us. Too long the church has interpreted repentance as a simple acceptance of "Jesus Christ as Lord and Savior," meaning that something called the soul will be saved in a life beyond this life. Honesty in this declaration (formula) is urgently needed. Repentance means accepting the *whole* gospel which includes the way and values of Jesus. It means turning to him who is at once Judge (obsessed with justice) and Savior (the giver of life). It means turning *to* Him, and turning *from* a society whose head is empty, whose heart is sick, and whose hands drip with innocent blood.

> When they curse you, return
> a blessing.
> When they ask a mile,
> go two.
> When they hate you,
> love them.
>
> God,
> it's so hard
> to live
> by the gospel.

The Meaning in Praise

Philippians 4:4

Henry H. Mitchell

There are two great disappointments facing Americans as they reflect on the ideals that gave birth to the nation. One is the fact that the American dream is as far away as ever for huge segments of the population, and the other is the fact that those who have achieved the affluence and privilege of the dream are still so joyless and threatened. This latter fact makes one wonder if there is something wrong with the dream—if we have hold of a false sense of what life is all about in the first place. Perhaps we should have been more critical

Henry H. Mitchell is a native of Columbus, Ohio, and now serves as Director of the Ecumenical Center for Black Church Studies in the Los Angeles area and as Adjunct Professor of Black Church Studies for the area's seminaries. He is a graduate of Lincoln University, Union Theological Seminary, and California State University, and received the Th.D. from Southern California School of Theology at Claremont. He has served as Dean of the chapel and instructor in English at North Carolina Central University, held posts with the Northern California Baptist Convention, was pastor of two churches in California, and was the first occupant of the Martin Luther King Chair in Black Studies at Colgate-Rochester Divinity School/Bexley Hall/ Crozer Theological Seminary. Author of many articles, he has published two books, *Black Preaching* and *Black Belief.* The American Baptist Seminary of the West at Covina honored him with the D.D.

of our quiet assumptions about life much sooner than we were.

For instance, human beings are referred to as *Homo sapiens,* mankind, the knowers, or the wise. Descartes made the famous statement, *"Cogito ergo sum,"* which carries the idea a bit further by saying that "I think, therefore I am." Summed up in these sayings is the subtle but towering error of Western culture: that thinking and scheming, necessary as they are, constitute the *chief* distinguishing feature, and indeed, the very end of persons.

Closely related to mental effort as the glory of human existence is the physical effort that thinking directs—in business, industry, finance, and government. There is a Protestant work ethic abroad which suggests that the chief end of humanity is to work, which may also include waging war. Western civilization's history, from before Beowulf to the current Boston riots, emphasizes a series of muscular and mechanical maneuvers to produce things and to impose one's will on the desired territories. Now, of course, work is necessary, but the error lies in seeking first the kinds of kingdoms which can be achieved by "muscle."

When I was a boy, I learned a creedal statement about chief ends. It went something like this: "The chief end of man [persons] is to glorify God and to enjoy him forever."

Paul made another statement which is in accord with it when he said: "Rejoice in the Lord always: and again I say, Rejoice" (Philippians 4:4, KJV). All of this meshes beautifully with my own African-American heritage in which, to use Dr. James A. Joseph's phrase, humankind should be referred to as *Homo festivus,* man, the celebrator. Novel as it might seem, even slaves lived up to that definition quite literally.

I say novel, because right away the question will be raised as to what on earth African-Americans have to celebrate compared to their fellow citizens. Why should blacks be the leading celebrators when there is so much yet to be done before they can claim the American dream? Well, the answer is easy once you can bring yourself to agree with Paul's unconditional commandment about perpetual rejoicing—praising God *all* the time. It has searching implications about the very meaning of life, and I think it's high time everybody started thinking of themselves in these primitive, but profound, terms of *Homo festivus.*

We should celebrate all the time, first of all, because just being alive is worthy of gratitude to God. Just to think the opposite is a self-fulfilling prophecy. We miss the joy of *being* because we rush beyond it to *having* and thoughts about *getting*. The blessings of which we are only partially conscious can hardly be expected to bring appropriate joy. Whatever we do or do not have, *we are!* Praise God!

One of Dr. Martin Luther King's favorite sermon themes is thanks to God for the leavings—for what's left. How could one who has lost two sons and a wife dream of such a topic? Well, he'd been preaching it all along, and he just leaned on it, and it sustained him. Unless we simply wish to cease to be, the goodness of life under God should be affirmed in rejoicing, unconditionally, and continually.

That's what black folks have done, literally. They have thanked God for just being. The traditional prayer heard from coast to coast in the churches of the black masses does just this, with poetic beauty and an unconscious depth:

> Lord, I want to thank you this morning that my bed was not my cooling board. I want to thank you that your guardian angels watched over me whilst I slumbered and slept, and this morning you touched me with your finger of love and I awoke in my right mind.

Some folks take simple survival for granted, assuming that life requires more than a fairly healthy body and being clothed in one's right mind. They feel that if God doesn't give that "more," life isn't really worth living and certainly not worthy of thanks and rejoicing. And that's too bad, for people who slip into this pattern are the losers. They have missed the first and fundamental fact of the unqualified blessing of existence under God, a great blessing recognized all too often only by paraplegics and others with handicaps that strip them down to such bare essentials.

The slaves who first prayed that prayer-poetry were simply following a celebrative cultural heritage brought with them from Africa. No slave master could have convinced them to affirm the goodness of being; they had known and believed it for centuries. But it was a stroke of religious genius that they kept the faith. By doing so they created their own living space—the atmosphere in which their souls lived, entirely apart from the omnipresent oppression. Bodies were beaten, but celebrating souls were out of reach. In the integrity of their own internal climate of rejoicing just to be living, they were able to maintain their humanity and their will not only to survive, but also to be free.

Many slave narratives mention the fact that workers in the fields were known to feel compelled to praise God a while (often in secret, for fear of brutal punishment) after working days of twelve or more hours. They would gather in a "praise house" (African term) or sneak away to a brush arbor to praise God before going to their cabins to eat and rest. The unbelievable horror of their lives was relieved by moments of celebration focused on the simple fact that they were alive and in fellowship, albeit in chains.

The things people achieve may be praiseworthy, but our celebration will be mere nationalistic propaganda unless we praise God for that more important part which he alone can give. "We hold these truths to be self-evident that all men are endowed *by their Creator* with inalienable rights. . . ." It is these God-given recesses of reality, beyond the reach of tyranny and bigotry, which blacks still celebrate. They have not the same temptations to "presumptuous sins" (Psalm 19:13), but theirs is a righteousness which must be sought by all persons of all classes and cultures if they would discover invulnerable and eternal meaning and joy in life.

However, the mystical meaning—the control of one's soul space—does not exhaust the topic of unceasing praise. The mechanical mentality bent on cause-and-effect must surely see that what we celebrate is also what we teach our young. Nothing is so well learned by our children as that which is lifted up in joyous, and even ecstatic, observance. African children today still retain fantastic collections of wise and religious sayings without having been taught them formally, simply because they have sung and danced them and heard them told in the numerous celebrations which punctuate their life cycle.

In America, if our chief heroes are warriors, our children will learn violence above all else. If our gratitude is poured out for the power to dominate and strip other nations of their resources so we can maintain a much higher living standard, the lesson of selfish desire and the wanton imbalance of material blessings will not be lost on our youth. But if we are true to America's heritage of joy for the spiritual potential of a land with religious liberty, enjoying a pluralism of faith expressions, then that, too, will be a part of the inevitable lesson to succeeding generations.

There is, again, a traditional black prayer which says sincerely:

> Whilst I am knee-bent and body-bowed,
> I want to thank you, Lord,
> That I can pick and choose
> My own praying ground.

This was not mere poetry. There was a time inside these two hundred years of America's "freedom" when blacks were beaten and even killed for praying and preaching. Such freedom as they now enjoy, though appreciably less than the national norm, is well worthy of thanksgiving. To lift up such liberty in thanks all over the land would surely increase the narrow variety of believers who have occupied the White House. When the American people properly praise God for the soul liberty in the Constitution, they may also in fact revive a crucial and God-given but endangered human right, a part of the American dream.

So celebration focuses on the affirmation of being, rightly praising God for the gift of life itself. In so doing it creates an inner climate of spiritual joy, but it also teaches the values lifted up and implants them indelibly on the minds of the young. The clincher on this idea of rejoicing in the Lord all the time, however, is something "out of this world." You see, praise is the perpetual project of all eternity:

> When we've been there ten thousand years,
> Bright shining as the sun,
> We've no less days to sing God's praise
> Than when we first begun.

The things we say about heaven are not mere "pie in the sky." When slaves sang that they were going to "put on my shoes, and going to shout all over God's heaven," they were making a firm judgment, not only about praise, but also about the shoes they should have been issued to work in here. The best we can say about heaven, for accuracy, can only be an extension of the highest we know here. When we reverse the process and start back from the stanza of "Amazing Grace" or the spiritual, it becomes abundantly evident that we are both underpraising God and missing the heavenly joy that comes with it. And that is to say nothing of pitifully preparing ourselves for an eternity of praising God.

Praise and celebration, then, are not just the childish outpouring of a primitive people; such rejoicing is the very will of God concerning everybody (1 Thessalonians 5:16). Here, as well as hereafter, the ecstasy of rejoicing in the Lord can give meaning to life, lifting up its most important aspects and teaching them to oncoming generations. And it will give us good practice for "shouting all over God's heaven."

I keep so busy praisin' my Jesus,
Keep so busy praisin' my Jesus,
Keep so busy praisin' my Jesus,
Ain't got time to die.

'Cause it takes all o' my time
Just to praise my Jesus,
All o' my time to praise my Lord;
If I don't praise Him, the rocks gonna cry out
Glory an' honor! Glory an' honor!
Ain't got time to die.

The Cross in the Marketplace

Mark 8:34-38

Foy Valentine

This is the age
Of the half-read page.
And the quick hash
And the mad dash.
The bright night
With the nerves tight.
The plane hop
And the brief stop.
The lamp tan
In a short span.

Foy Valentine, a native of Texas, is the Executive Secretary of the Christian Life Commission of the Southern Baptist Convention. He is a graduate of Baylor University and received his Th.M. and Th.D. degrees from Southwestern Baptist Theological Seminary in Fort Worth, Texas. He has been a Baptist Student Director, pastor of the First Baptist Church, Gonzales, Texas, and Director of the Texas Baptist Christian Life Commission. He has served as co-chairman of the Baptist World Alliance's Commission on Religious Liberty and Human Rights, member of the Board of Trustees of the Americans United for Separation of Church and State, and a member of the Baptist Joint Committee on Public Affairs. He is the author of six books, including *Where the Action Is, Citizenship for Christians, Christian Faith in Action,* and *Believe and Behave.* William Jewell College conferred the D.D. degree upon him in 1966.

> The Big Shot
> In a good spot.
> And the brain strain
> And the heart pain
> And the cat naps
> Till the spring snaps—
> And the fun's done! [1]

Virginia Brasier

This may not be great poetry, but it is a reasonably accurate portrayal of the age in which we live.

This age, like every age, is an age that tries men's souls. It is an age of dry eyes, hard noses, and cold feet. It was once just at sixes and sevens, but suddenly it finds itself at twelves and fourteens. It follows the wind; it embraces the darkness; it loves a vacuum. Its beatitude is, "Blessed are the smooth, for they shall never be wrinkled."

It indulges in a myopic narcissism over its own wonderful works—split atoms and a few tons of tin which it has hung on nothing. It proposes fantastically expensive voyages into space without the foggiest notion as to what to do with the space it already has. It overeats, overdrinks, overworks, and overplays so that its immoderation is known to all. It walks delicately, thinks slovenly, lives dully, sleeps poorly, and wakes up tired.

It is better acquainted with name brands than it is with firebrands. It knows more about bombs than it does about Bibles. It understands the infernal possibilities of hydrogen better than the infinite potentialities of heaven. It actually talks more about calories than it does about Christ. It has grown fat feeding on fingernails.

It is the age of grown people wrapped in intellectual swaddling clothes, of Christians who spoon one another lukewarm pabulum in preference to the meat of strong doctrine. This is the age of the Beefed-up Big Brother and of 1984 before 1980. It is a gadget-filled paradise suspended in a hell of insecurity.

It is the age of calculated irrelevance in political campaigns—and in many an ecclesiastical empire. It is the age of the fast buck, the goof-off, the fixed price, the half-done job, the accommodated moral standard, the proximate solution, the interim ethic, a bottomless relativism, and the "new morality" which is as old as the serpent in the Garden. It fills its tank with high-octane hypocrisy from which it gets understandably poor mileage. It loves the simple purity of well-ordered confusion. It is as far from real repentance for its sin as Oral

Roberts is from the Mayo Clinic, and it knows as little about true faith in Jesus Christ as a downtown tomcat knows about *Home Life* magazine.

It knows intimately the heavy legacy of hatred, and it still responds to the demagogue's intoxicating oratory. It experiences great difficulty in distinguishing between the white horse of victory and the pale horse of death, so vast is its confusion.

It has a limited vision of poverty and an unlimited poverty of vision. It is like ancient Israel of whom it was said, "The word of the Lord was rare in those days; there was no frequent vision" (1 Samuel 3:1, RSV). It is the age of cheap grace where sinners have been called to Christ without being called to bring forth social fruits "meet for repentance."

Its loins are girt about with half-truth; it bears the breastplate of self-righteousness; its feet are shod with the bad news of preparation for war; it clutches the shield of doubt; it wears the helmet of damnation; and it wields the sword of the flesh.

In this time of agonizing reappraisal when the question "What's wrong?" is on a vast multitude of lips both in the nation and in our Christian fellowship, let us ask first: "Where is God?" "Who am I?" "What shall we do?"

When Bildad, Eliphaz, and Zophar were giving their inadequate answers, Job was asking the important questions. Perhaps this age also can profit by asking again the important questions: "Where is God?" "Who am I?" "What shall we do?"

WHERE IS GOD?

God is in history effecting human salvation. He is in creation, in Adam, in Noah, in Abraham, Isaac, and Jacob, in Moses, in Isaiah, and in Amos, in the Law and the Prophets, in the cradle of Bethlehem, and on the cross at Calvary. But God is not only in ancient history; he is in modern history as well—in the Reformation, in the nailing of Martin Luther's ninety-five theses to the door of the Castle Church in Wittenberg, in the three intrepid little sailboats of Christopher Columbus, in Schweitzer's hospital compound, in Africa's bold step into the twentieth century, in the halls of the United Nations where people are trying to learn the gray art of shouting at one another instead of the black art of shooting at one another, in today's human affairs, conference rooms, marketplaces, and crossroads. God is not simply There and Then. God is Here and Now, the great "I am that I am," beyond history, before history, over history, under history, and in history. And Christ's gospel of redemption, his good news of salvation, came not only to the shepherds in the Judean hills in an agrarian world two thousand years ago. His gospel has come to this age also.

History is not just something unpleasant that happens to other folks. History happens to everybody. And history has now happened to us. There is no justification for our standing here shuffling our feet and wringing our hands and crying and cutting ourselves with knives and neurotically hunting scapegoats. God is in history. Our sovereign God is in history effecting our salvation; and we ought to feel a wonderful security, a glorious liberty, and a peace that passes all understanding in this knowledge. As the winds of change blow with their devastating fury across the face of all the earth, let us trust the God who is in history, for he is in our history also. If we are true to God, he will not forsake us; and if we are not true to him, no amount of histrionics will throw the hounds of heaven off our trail.

Where is God? God is in Christ reconciling the world unto himself. To say that God is in Christ is to affirm that Jesus Christ our Lord is the Word by whom the worlds were made, the Lamb slain from the foundation of the world, the Messiah of Old Testament prophecy, in the fullness of time a perfect man and every whit a man, and the Author, Sustainer, and Finisher of our faith. To say that God in Christ is reconciling the world to himself is to say that Christ's reconciling work is past, present, and future. It is past in the sense that Christ has reconciled the believing sinner and the heavenly Father. It is present in the sense that men and women, through Christ, are being reconciled to their estranged families, separated parents, distrusting children, and alienated neighbors. It is future in the sense that we shall know complete conformity to Christ who loved us and gave himself for us, for Christ who has begun the work of grace in us will assuredly complete it in his own time. Jesus Christ is not just King of Kings and Lord of Lords in Handel's *Messiah.* He is King of Gerald Ford and Lord of Mao Tse-Tung. He is King of Harold Wilson and Lord of Castro.

Our world has had a great fall and not all of the Free World's horses or all of communism's men can put it together again. This is the work of God who is in Christ reconciling the world unto himself.

Where is God? God is in the church. Spurgeon said, "I do not believe in salvation outside the pale of the church." And if we will not hear Spurgeon, then let us hear Jesus who said, "He that believeth and is baptized shall be saved" (Mark 16:16, KJV) and again "Upon this rock I will build my church; and the gates of hell shall not prevail against it" (Matthew 16:18, KJV). To say that God and his great salvation are one thing and church membership quite another thing, a mere optional matter for individuals to take or leave, is to inject into revealed religion an element of isolated, prickly individualism which fractures the gospel and fragments the New Testament. The church is the body of Christ, the bride of Christ, the building of Christ. It is the *ecclesia* of God distinguished by fellowship, service, and proclamation—*koinonia, diakonia,* and *kerygma*—brothering, helping, and preaching. As all people must have community or be less than human, so Christians must have the church or perish. It is infinitely more important, moreover, for the people of God to *be* the church than it is for them simply to attend church, build the church, support the church, give to the church, or serve the church. Christians who grasp this idea that they *are* the church understand that Christianity must be demonstrated before it is declared, that it must be done before it can be taught, that it must be practiced before it is preached.

Where is God? God is in history; God is in Christ; and God is in the church.

WHO AM I?

At the graveside of Willy Loman in Arthur Miller's *Death of a Salesman,* one of the characters standing by says with rare discernment, "He never knew who he was."[2] Is not this the essence of tragedy? The need to know who we are, to be somebody, to have a name, is as deep as life. In these times there are many hindrances to self-identification: the uprooting of families by moves so frequent that sociologists say there has never before in history been as much voluntary migration as there is in the United States today, the lack of leisure, the paucity of sanctuary, and the absence of father and family and friends and kinfolks to help provide the answer to the great question, "Who am I?"

Who am I? I am a man made in the image of God, after his spiritual, rational, and moral likeness. As a man, I am made in the image of God. It is because of this that I must insist that I am not America's man or the South's man or capitalism's man or free enterprise's man or labor's man or management's man or the

Democrat's man or the Republican's man or Ford's man or Goldwater's man or the Convention's man or the Commission's man but God's man.

Who am I? I am a Christian man, "bought, and at a price!" (1 Corinthians 6:20, J.B. Phillips). Because Christ died for me and because he loves me, I have infinite value as does every other human being on earth. It is in encounter with the living God through repentance and faith in Jesus Christ as Lord that I become a whole man, and it is only after this encounter that I can tell you, really, who I am; and it is in this encounter alone that humankind in quest of its true identity can come to itself, find its name, and be somebody.

Who am I? I am responsible. I am a responsible Christian man. Every moral decision of my life I am constrained to make in the light of who I am. It is as a responsible Christian man that I must make decisions about family life, race relations, daily work, citizenship, and specific moral issues which always dog the feet of a moral person. My basic concern is not that Christians should combat successfully the specific family problems of teenage marriages, the breakdown of authority in the home, divorce, and aging, but that Christians *should want to* confront these issues in the mind and spirit of Christ. My first concern is not that Christians should kill Jim Crow, but that they *should want to* kill Jim Crow; not that Christians should transform politics, but that they *should want to* transform politics; not that they should conquer alcohol, but that they *should want to* conquer alcohol; not that they should defeat gambling, but that they *should want to* defeat gambling—*because of who they are.* When God says, "Be ye holy; for I am holy" (1 Peter 1:16, KJV), he is actually saying, "Be my people, for I am your God." Be righteous because God is righteous. Be right because God is right. Be responsible because God is responsible.

WHAT SHALL WE DO?

We are in no position to ask, "What shall we do?" until we have first asked, "Where is God?" and "Who am I?" When these two prior questions have been asked and answered, however, then the one, great, overpowering question remaining is, "What shall we do?" Having become, by God's grace, the people we ought to be, we can by the power of his might do the work we ought to do.

As George MacLeod said:

I am recovering the claim that Jesus was not crucified in a cathedral between two candles, but on a cross between two thieves; on the town garbage-heap; at a crossroad so cosmopolitan that they had to write his title in Hebrew and in Latin and in Greek (or shall we say in English, in Bantu and in Afrikaans?); at the kind of place where cynics talk smut, and thieves curse, and soldiers gamble. Because that is where He died. And that is what He died about. And that is where churchmen should be and what churchmanship should be about.[3]

What shall we do? We shall renew our vows to God. We shall not forsake the assembling of ourselves together as the manner of some is. We shall be good stewards of all that we have and are and hope to be. We shall preach the gospel. We shall not wince at the scandal of the cross. We shall be swimmers against tides.

We shall match our disenchantment with the present age with a patient effort to change it. We shall add our Christian salt to the fresh, red meat that is our present world lest the maggots of mammon infect and ruin it. We shall shine our lights in a dim and gloomy world where without them people would continue to stumble piteously and fall painfully in the dark.

Knowing that the disembodied, unformed Word is no Word at all, we shall again let the Word be flesh so that the love of God is expressed through our changed lives in a language others can understand. We shall recognize that social involvement is not an optional matter of ethical obedience but a condition of being in communion with God at all. We shall understand that to be hid with God in Christ is not to wallow in glossolalia but to be rightly involved in community. We shall quit singing, "Far away the noise of strife upon my ear is falling. . . . Safe am I within the castle of God's word retreating . . . For I am dwelling in Beulah Land" and start singing, "Rescue the perishing; care for the dying; snatch them in pity from sin and the grave," and "Where Cross the Crowded Ways of Life."

We shall return to a concern for people with the assurance that as we do, our religion will burst gloriously into new life. We shall reaffirm our conviction that the biblical ideals of one man and one woman joined together for life in the bonds of holy matrimony, the sacredness of sex, discipline in the home, respect for parents, and the importance of persons over things are permanently valid ideals. We shall raise the cross over the hearthstone, over the kitchen table, over the family room, over the marital bed, and over the baby bed.

We shall remember that Paul nearly always commenced his epistles with piety and climaxed them with politics.

We shall know again the heady, hearty, holy thrill of moral

leadership. We shall stand in the bow of the ship as it cuts its way into the uncharted sea of a new world order.

We shall not mythologize the pivotal point of the Christian gospel: that the essence of the heavenly Father's majesty is Jesus Christ's glorious humanity. We shall feed the hungry, heal the brokenhearted, set at liberty them that are bruised, clothe the naked, release the prisoners from bondage, and preach the gospel to the poor. We shall recover the fullness of the gospel. We shall acknowledge the claim of Christ on all of life. We shall own him Lord.

What shall we do? We shall raise again the cross in the marketplace, for this is where God is, this is who I am, and this is what we must do.

The Rosedown Woman

Matthew 25:31-45

Clyde E. Fant

Most of us have gotten too old and dignified by now to be able to admit it, but when we were growing up, we probably did a lot of daydreaming—especially those of us who grew up in the Great Comic Book Era. I remember that I loved to read comic books and that I always envied all those mythical figures that were able to do anything they wanted to—leaping over buildings at a single bound, outrunning speeding locomotives, and other useful things.

More than any of the others, though, I really envied the boy who

Clyde E. Fant, a native Texan, is pastor of the First Baptist Church, Richardson, Texas. Formerly he served as Professor of Preaching at Southwestern Baptist Theological Seminary in Fort Worth, Texas. He is a graduate of Baylor University and received his B.D., M.Div., and Th.D. degrees from Southwestern Baptist Theological Seminary. As a Fulbright Scholar, he studied at Eberhard-Karls University, Tübingen, Germany, and later did post-doctoral research at the Institute for Hermeneutics, Tübingen, Germany. He is the author of *Preaching for Today, Bonhoeffer: Worldly Preaching,* coauthor of the 13-volume set, *Twenty Centuries of Great Preaching: An Encyclopedia of Preaching,* and coeditor of *Contemporary Christian Trends.* He has served on many community and denominational committees. He received the Venting Award from Southwestern Seminary and was the 1975 convention speaker for the European Baptist Convention.

could say "Shazam" and turn himself into Captain Marvel. I thought that had to be the greatest thing in the world, just simply to say whatever magic word it took and instead of being a ninety-seven-pound Billy Batson weakling, suddenly I would be Captain Marvel.

During that summertime when we were having terrible polio epidemics and everybody was scared to death, I remember my mother insisting, "You've got to take a nap every afternoon!" I was mortified. "Mother, I'm too old to take a nap every afternoon!" But I wasn't. (I'm now back to taking naps again in the afternoon. I have one in mind this afternoon.) So I would lie there on the bed and look out at the big cottonwood tree that made my hayfever and asthma so bad, and sometimes when I knew nobody could hear me, I would whisper, "Shazam." It never worked, really, except in my imagination; but that never mattered, I guess, because it didn't kill the daydream.

But I must not have been alone by myself in that, because there have always been people who are looking for some magic word that will change their lives and magically transform them from what they are to what they want to be.

We've all sung the hymn "Onward, Christian Soldiers." We probably didn't know the music was written by Arthur Sullivan—and for that matter, we probably didn't know who Arthur Sullivan was—unless we connected his name with Gilbert and Sullivan. Arthur Sullivan was a frustrated man. He didn't want to be remembered for all those popular operettas like *The Mikado* and *The Pirates of Penzance;* he wanted to be known as a great composer of classical music. He was very frustrated by what he was.

Lewis Carroll, really known only because of his writing of *Alice in Wonderland* and *Through the Looking Glass,* was always bitterly disappointed that he was never recognized as a great mathematician. And even Beatrix Potter, who was the "mother" of *Peter Rabbit*—the woman who wrote all the stories about Peter Cottontail—was bitter, especially late in her life, because she was never recognized as a great writer but simply as a woman who wrote children's stories.

You see, their problem was becoming something. Once they became what they were, they couldn't be anything else.

I had a teacher in high school who always used to say, "Be careful when you choose a book to read, because if you read one book, it automatically means you can't read another book." I always thought that was really stupid (which meant I didn't understand it). But it's funny that I've remembered what she said all these years. If you choose one thing, you've automatically chosen against something else. And that is giving a lot of people serious problems.

Right now restlessness with vocations is at epidemic levels. People want to be something else. They are not happy being what they are, and an enormous amount of change is going on today. A survey by the American Management Association revealed that 52 percent of the managers contacted found their work to be unsatisfying. Nearly 50 percent of them have considered changing or have actually changed their occupation in the six years preceding the study.

Everybody's doing something else. I know a very successful M.D. who is going back to law school, and I am positive somewhere there is a lawyer who is going to medical school.

There are famous models who say, "Modeling is not significant, I want to be a movie star"; and there are movie stars who say, "This is not significant, I want to be on Broadway." There are people on Broadway who say, "This is not significant, I want to be in politics." There are people in politics who say, "This is not significant; I don't know what I'm doing, or why. I want to be in business." And there are people in business who say, "Making money is not significant; I want to make a contribution to the arts or politics." Most of us, to one degree or another, are infected with this insecurity. What we are doing just isn't significant.

Allow me to state for you Fant's First Law (I never had another one, so this is my first): *Nothing is so important as when you are not it.* When you are *not* something, it's important; and nothing is ever as important as something you're not and maybe can't get to be. But when you become it, it ceases to be important.

Did you ever notice that? It's important to get this, or to be this, or to be chosen to be this—until you get it. (Remember how you felt the day after you were elected vice-president of the sophomore class?) Once *you* touch it, somehow it begins to diminish in importance. Most of us seem to feel, "If *I'm* it, it *can't* be important!" And this says a lot about what we think about ourselves. So we are restless; we've just got to do something else. But what?

I don't know that I can help you very much to think through why we feel this way, but at least I want to tell you what I think. It seems to me there are many reasons why so many of us are miserable being us.

In the first place, we are living in a time of greatly increased options. There is just simply more to do. If you were a serf working a little plot of ground that your father, your grandfather, and your great-great-grandfather, back to time immemorial, had labored over, you wouldn't be sitting around thinking, "What in the world am I going to do with my life?" You'd know what you are going to do with your life—dig out potatoes and die right there on those forty acres. Or you might think about going off and killing the king, but you wouldn't think about changing vocations. We just simply see more options now, and we become unhappy. Not only is the grass greener across the fence, but also we can look over into more pastures than we used to be able to see. We're always meeting somebody who seems to have the most fascinating career. "Oh, that would be so interesting! I wish I had only known about that, but I'm stuck. Here I am, where I am, and it's too late to do anything about it."

When my boy went off to college, we had a good long talk. One of the things we talked about was what he was going to study. In typical conversation he asked, "Dad, how in the world does anybody know what to be? There are so many different things that you can do. There are so many jobs. How can you possibly even know about all the jobs—much less know which one to pick out?" I wish I could reflect my snappy solution to you, but I didn't have one.

It is also a time when we see so much change around us that we're positive that change has got to be the answer. Americans are changing everything they've got at the most rapid rate you can imagine. It isn't just our cars we're trading in faster than anybody else in the world. We're trading in our wives and husbands faster than anybody else. We're trading our jobs. We're trading our interests. We're trading everything we've got, because we are convinced that if we can change something, it's got to be better.

Pain always leads to change. Put your hand on a hot stove sometime and think that over. You know you're going to jerk your hand back just as quickly as you can. When our life pain begins to increase, we begin to look for some way to change our environment. That's normal, and it's probably pretty healthy sometimes. But is change always the answer? If it is, then we are certainly condemned to a lifetime of endless restlessness.

This is also an age of object satisfaction. People have learned that it's fun to have things and that they can find satisfaction through objects. We've all got more toys now than anybody who ever lived on the face of the earth. I'm not talking about the kids. Most of the toys that are bought are bought by adults; toys for boys—big boys who have got enough money to buy them. We find that by buying new toys—and sometimes pretty expensive toys—we can be amused for awhile. This is object satisfaction. But it doesn't last very long, and we've got to find other objects to amuse us ... until we run out of ideas and dreams and hope, all at the same time. Suicide sometimes terminates the search.

We are living under the promise of education, as well. Education has promised us a great deal. I'm not so sure that education has not promised a bit more than it can deliver. Of course you've got to know something. But isn't it possible that one reason we are so miserably unhappy is that we thought once we went through the educational program, the world would deliver to us not only the income but also the satisfaction that we wanted? And we have found out that we just can't sit back on our diplomas and wait for life to bring us happiness.

People are going back to school in record numbers. I'm not altogether convinced that this new increase in adult education is really a passion for learning. It would be a wonderful thing, I suppose, if it was. But I think a great deal of the back-to-school movement is not entirely composed of a healthy desire to do something creative and interesting. I am wondering if many people did not fixate somewhere back in the past at a school grade where they found some meaning in the excitement of the crowd and the group and the activities, and they've just never found that since. They want to try to go back and get in that environment that was so stimulating and so interesting and so meaningful.

We are also living in a time of fatigue with crowds. We are worn out with crowds. You remember the last time you went to a state fair, walked down the midway, and got bumped by everybody? How about the last time you were on the blessed freeway—our divine Central Expressway at the "Hour of Power" when all the machines are out there and everyone is gunning his car, trying to get in front of you? You fight that crowd, day after day, and you come back and you say, "I don't want to see anybody!"

I was reading about a famous author who had some friends visiting from the northernmost part of North Dakota. They had just sat down at the table for dinner when the doorbell rang. The host said, " Oh, no, not somebody coming to see us right at mealtime!" He got up and went to the door, and when he came back after an abrupt conversation, he found that his guests were absolutely shocked. He said it was obvious that there was nothing as profane that he could possibly have done as to fail to show courtesy to a visitor who came to his door. His friends said, "Where we live, we are so glad to hear anybody knock on the door that we just can't imagine not being delighted to have visitors come around."

But that's not the world we live in. We live in a world of walls. We've gotten restless with our contact with people. We are too exhausted to get involved with people. And right there is the problem. And right there the solution begins. And right there I want to tell you about the Rosedown Woman.

I was down in southern Louisiana recently and went out to the once great plantation called Rosedown. If you have ever been on a tour of any of the antebellum homes in the South, you have probably been to Rosedown. It is the classic southern mansion—curving walks, enormous oak trees, fantastic gardens, and a magnificent house. You are met at the door by three rather elderly ladies who show you through the home. The first woman points you to the second, and the second begins to tell you about the living room and the library.

As she began to tell us about the house, I noticed that she wasn't looking at us. She was just looking past us—not out the window, but just toward the window. Her eyes were fixed like they are when somebody is a million miles away, and she went on with her spiel. She said, "Now you will notice over there a very beautiful thing to my left which sits up here on the shelf." She said, "This dates way back in the family," and so on, and so on. And I wondered what in the world it must be like to spend each day, for more than twenty years, as each of these women has done, going through the same lines to the hundreds and thousands of strangers who have wandered through. And I thought, "You know, if that was my job, if I had to come in here every day and tell strangers about this house, I'd go crazy. I just couldn't stand it."

But the preoccupied lady downstairs was not the Rosedown Woman. The Rosedown Woman was upstairs. She was as different from the first woman as night and day. She showed us the dining room and the children's rooms. She was smiling and she was alert and she was alive and there was expression on her face. She began to tell us about the big shoo-fly, the enormous fan that hung over the table, where you pulled the silken cord and the big thing flapped back and forth and scared all the flies off the food. And she would name each of the items of the house. And she called a little boy to her and said,

"Son, would you like to pull the rope and work the fan?" Was he excited! He pulled on the thing, and it flapped back and forth.

Then we went to the children's room, and she singled out one of the very small children, and she said, "Did you ever sleep in a baby bed as big as that one?" And the little child said, "No!" We all got caught up in it. A friend of mine, a professor of voice, got so carried away listening to her name each of those things with a French name, that he pointed to a little settee and said, "What did they call that thing?" She said, "What?" Frank said, "That little settee." She looked at him for a minute and she said, "I think they called that a bench." Everybody laughed except Frank. He didn't.

She had a terrific time, and she told us good-bye, and we felt real good. When I got outside, I thought, "What an incredible difference between those two women! They have been there the same length of time. The difference is, the one upstairs really loves her job." And then I thought about that; and I thought, "No, that's not so. She doesn't love her job. She loves the *people.* She gets involved with the people who come her way. She's got the same square footage to work. She's got the same old spiel that she's supposed to parrot out to people. But she doesn't do that. Every exchange of guests that comes through, incredibly, she makes personally involved with her life. She actually gives something of her personality and, even as ridiculous as it sounds, of her love to those strangers who come through where she lives."

And that's really the answer. Because God is in that.

Maybe we're ready for a little Scripture now:

When the Son of man shall come in his glory, and all the holy angels with him, then shall he sit upon the throne of his glory:

And before him shall be gathered all nations: and he shall separate them one from another, as a shepherd divideth his sheep from the goats:

And he shall set the sheep on his right hand, but the goats on the left.

Then shall the King say unto them on his right hand, Come, ye blessed of my Father, inherit the kingdom prepared for you from the foundation of the world:

For I was an hungred, and ye gave me meat: I was thirsty, and ye gave me drink: I was a stranger, and ye took me in:

Naked and ye clothed me: I was sick, and ye visited me: I was in prison, and ye came unto me.

Then shall the righteous answer him, saying, Lord, when saw we thee an hungred, and fed thee? or thirsty, and gave thee drink?

When saw we thee a stranger, and took thee in? or naked, and clothed thee?

Or when saw we thee sick, or in prison, and came unto thee?

And the King shall answer and say unto them, Verily I say unto you, Inasmuch as ye have done it unto one of the least of these my brethren, ye have done it unto me (Matthew 25:31-45, KJV).

Whosoever will save his life shall lose it:

and whosoever will lose his life for my sake shall find it (Matthew 16:25, KJV).

No doubt there are some people who need to change vocation. I am positive that's so. It's possible to get into work that really isn't you, and you need to be in something else to be satisfied. But you and I both know that much of the time that's not the answer. Much of the time the reason for the purposelessness and the meaninglessness of our lives is not the environment on the outside. It's the environment on the inside. It's because we're just going through the paces now. We're not seeing anybody. We're just giving our spiel, "On the shelf behind and to the left, there is an important thing." And that's all there is to life. We get up in the morning and we get out in the crowds, and we get in the machinery and we work with the machinery. We never see the people. We're living an inhuman life—going through the paces.

And all the while, we're saying, "Won't somebody love me? Won't somebody give me something? Won't somebody say something nice about me?" We're holding life by the throat, like a child clutching a puppy by the neck. And we're holding it so tightly to ourselves that finally we hold nothing else in our hands but its poor, dead body. Until we come to the Christ with our lives—little, insignificant, daily lives—and hold them out and say, "Here. Here. You take it. Can you bring it back to life again?", we will go on living the life of the dead and the damned: restless, wandering, empty.

But how? How can he give us meaning? He isn't here anymore. We cannot follow him about the lake as his apostles did. Yet it is still the same. It is right before us, as it was before them, and we are as blind as they. In the selfish seeking to save our life, we're killing it. "Whoever seeks to save his life, shall lose . . . whoever loses his life, for my sake, finds." It is God that we need! *That* is meaning, and purpose, and assurance. However we define our craving, it is God that we need.

But where is he? Where, Lord? Where? Listen! "Unto the least of these . . . unto me!" "*I* was hungry . . . naked . . . in prison . . . and you came to *me*!" He *is* here—in them.

Most of us, I guess, have heard Tolstoy's story about Martin the cobbler who wanted to see God in a great vision. And God gave him a visitation in a strange way. But I'd like to change that story a bit and give you a contemporary parable that may speak more plainly to us.

There was once a man in Dallas who was an engineer for a large company. He loved God and he wanted to see God. He wanted to do something meaningful with his life, but he didn't know how. Every day he prayed, "God, show me your self." And he came to church every week, but he never saw God. He went to great meetings of Christians and listened to spectacular preaching, but he never saw God. And it seemed that his life had reached the bottom of despair. He prayed, "Lord, why will you not show me yourself?"

At work one day a young man, very young, came into his office. He had never seen him before. The young man said, "I work in your section here. I haven't been here very long. I'm having a lot of trouble. I don't really know what I'm doing about this particular problem, and they told me that if you would, you could help me."

Now the engineer was having a bad day. It was one of those days, you know. Everything had gone wrong. He was behind, way behind. People were on his back. He didn't have time enough to do what he needed to do, but he saw a look of trust—and a little bit of fear—in the eyes of the young man, and he said, "All right." And he began to help him. He spent longer than he meant to, most of the morning. But he saw a look of relief in the face of the young man when he stood up to leave, and then just before he left the office, he turned and said, "Say, maybe—maybe sometime you and your wife could come over to the apartment and have supper with my wife and me." He knew he never would, really, but he said, "Great! Maybe sometime we can do that."

The day went on and it got worse, not better. He was running late, way behind. As he was hurrying down through the office, he passed one of the older ladies just as she took a handkerchief out of her pocket and pressed it into the corners of her eyes. He stopped and said, "What's the matter, Martha? Can I help?" She told him about her daughter who lived so far away, with her baby who was real sick, so far away that she couldn't fly up there and see about the grandbaby that she loved. So he sat—longer than he meant to—and they talked. And when he got up, her tears were gone, and she said simply, "Thank you."

He had to work really late that night, later than ever. He thought to himself, "Well, at least the traffic will be gone off the freeway by now." It was dark when he went outside, and freezing cold. The wind was up, and he was tired and chilled. The parking lot was deserted except for one car in addition to his. And when he saw it, he thought, "Oh, no!" He was really hoping the man would say, "No, it's fine, I've got it taken care of." But the man didn't. He said, "Man, would you? If you could just run me up to the station, maybe I could get somebody to come back here. It looks like my battery is dead." And he thought to himself, *Supper is going to be as hard as a rock, and my wife is going to be harder than that when I get home.* But he said, "Okay, get in." He put him in the car and took him to the station, and when the man got out, he turned and looked at him for a long moment with a penetrating, pleased look; then shook hands and said brightly, "Good-bye!"

That night the engineer prayed again: "O God, why don't you show me yourself? Why don't you speak to me?" And then God spoke to him. He said, "I did, my son. Three times today, I came to you. Did you not know me? Did you not know me as the Christ child in the smooth face of the young man, alone, alone in a new world? In the tears of the woman, did you not see the suffering of my torn hands and side? In the man who needed someone's help, did you not hear my call? I did come unto you, and you blessed me."

And that night for the first time, he slept.

A prayer, now, for a life of purpose: "O Lord, God, we who spend most of our time looking for ourselves, and little of our time looking for you, help us to hear the Word of the Gospel, 'Inasmuch as you have done it unto one of the least of these, my brethren, you have done it unto me.' We know that the only ultimate meaning in life is in God, because all that we have perishes and is gone like a morning cloud, chaff from a threshing floor, smoke out of a chimney. None of the toys we have will last. None of that which we possess will ultimately be ours.

"Only the people whom we touch, only those who need you, only those whom through you we are able to bless, will accompany us into the kingdom. This is where God is. This is where our reward is—not only when we stand in the Day of Judgment with all of the holy angels surrounding us; not just then do we wait for our reward. But even now on earth the kingdom may come as thy will is done, and heaven may come around us even as it is around you, as we touch with hands that speak the name of Jesus, the healing compassion of Christ. That even as we offer a cup of cold water to an arid life, where it is done because of the love of Jesus and in his name, we know that it will not lose its reward.

"Teach us not to cling so fiercely to our own life that we kill it, but teach us to offer it freely unto others that we might offer it freely unto you, so that we might find in our own lives the deep satisfaction that we so desperately pray for. We thank you for the gift of abundant life, in Jesus' name. Amen."

On Overcoming Moral Fatigue

Isaiah 40:28-31

Samuel D. Proctor

We really do not need to know much else about the people the prophet Isaiah is confronting, for it is clear that they have been overcome with moral fatigue. But we cannot be overcome with moral fatigue; we must overcome it.

The term "moral fatigue" is used to characterize those who see little purpose to life, who feel that nothing is really worthwhile, who drag themselves out of one hour into the next, whose enthusiasm is spent, and who feel that the whole thing called life is nothing but "a

Samuel D. Proctor holds the Martin Luther King Memorial Chair as Professor of Education in the Graduate School of Rutgers University and is Senior Minister in the Abyssinian Baptist Church, New York City. He is a Virginian, an alumnus of Virginia Union University, Crozer Seminary, and Boston University, earning the doctorate in ethics from the latter. Additional graduate study was done at the University of Pennsylvania, Yale, and Harvard. He has served as President of Virginia Union University and North Carolina A & T State University. From 1964–1969 he held administrative positions with the Peace Corps in Nigeria and Washington, the National Council of Churches, the Office of Economic Opportunity, the Institute for Services to Education, and the University of Wisconsin. He is the author of *The Young Negro in America 1960–1980*. In 1964 he was awarded an Outstanding Alumnus Award at Boston University.

tale told by an idiot full of sound and fury, signifying nothing."

These majestic words of Isaiah are addressed to the Jewish exiles in Babylon, but their echo is heard across the ages by all of us who are overcome with moral fatigue. When the headlines tell of bribery on a global scale by trusted corporation presidents; government agencies violating the Constitution in bold and flagrant ways; a president and his vice-president run out of office for lying to the whole nation on network television; drugs available to high school students on a minute's notice; pornography staring at us from every airport newsstand; the national budget burdened with enormous expenditures for death and the end of mankind on planet Earth; the city where the democratic ideal was born and where black patriots first died for America's freedom engulfed in a nasty, name-calling racial war; the financial capital of the world begging for money to honor its debts; college graduates trained to do marvelous things selling hamburgers to pay their rent; and when there is a vacuum in moral and spiritual values being filled with all sorts of spine-tingling, star-gazing, empty ecstasy, we are left limp. We understand what Omar the tentmaker meant when he said in his Rubáiyát:

> Ah, Love! could you and I with him conspire
> To grasp this sorry Scheme of Things entire,
> Would not we shatter it to bits—and, then
> Re-mold it nearer to the heart's desire![1]

Well, that is one answer to moral fatigue, disgust, surrender, and cynical resignation. Another answer comes reverberating through the corridors of time from the prophet of ancient Israel:

> Have you not known? Have you not heard?
> The Lord is the everlasting God,
>   the Creator of the ends of the earth,
> He does not faint or grow weary,
>   his understanding is unsearchable.
> He gives power to the faint,
>   and to him who has no might he increases strength.
> Even youths shall faint and be weary,
>   and young men shall fall exhausted;
> but they who wait for the Lord shall renew their strength,
>   they shall mount up with wings like eagles,
> they shall run and not be weary,
>   they shall walk and not faint.
>   —Isaiah 40:28-31 (RSV)

There are three kinds of fatigue: first, there is physical fatigue.

We all know how that feels—forgetting first names, seeing things that are not there, driving through red lights, keeping a checkbook unbalanced, snapping at all and sundry! Physical fatigue causes one to spend lots of time on things that do not matter at all and little or no time on things that matter most. In order to pull out of this, all one needs is three good hot meals and ten hours' sleep. You will overcome physical fatigue.

Then, there is psychological fatigue. This is dangerous. It occurs when that person we would genuinely like to be gets too demanding, calls for too much discipline, too much thinking and choosing. We all have that best self of whom we are most proud. Human beings have the capacity to keep many *personae* in the wings, and we can adopt either one or the other as we choose. We are all a little schizoid, with several selves. But there is that best one that we all know too well. We have embraced that *persona* every now and then, but it is tough to maintain that rule. It calls for some privacy, prayer, and introspection; it calls for forgiving our friends for minor insults and our enemies for major attacks; it calls for reading widely and well and looking for good company with edifying conversation; it calls for waiting on God in the beauty of holiness; it calls for climbing our Mount Carmels and waiting for the still, small voice, and walking through our Gethsemanes saying, "Not my will but thine be done." And when we cannot meet these conditions, we lapse into one of those other lesser *personae,* one of our worse selves. This is psychological fatigue, when the psyche (soul!) we really prefer has run out of spiritual energy.

> Even youths shall faint and be weary,
>   and young men shall fall exhausted;
> but they who wait for the Lord shall
>   renew their strength,
> they shall mount up with wings like eagles,
> they shall run and not be weary,
>   they shall walk and not faint.
>   —Isaiah 40:30-31 (RSV)

And then, there is moral fatigue. This occurs when one sees no sense in making an effort, when the whole idea of decency has lost its appeal. We become numb, callous, and hardhearted. We no longer flinch at the cracking sound of a pistol shot or shudder at mass murder. We flip our newspaper from war, to gossip, to football, to homicide, to comics, to bribery, to big-time corruption, to unemployment and back to other small intermittent wars, with women and babies running and screaming under the screeching, eerie whistling of a bomber, darting through the moon rays of the night. And we never twitch an eyelash. Routine stuff! After a while it gets to you, and your prayers get stuck in your throat. You cease caring.

Psalm 42 is the cry of a man almost lapsing into moral fatigue. "As the hart panteth after the water brooks, so panteth my soul after thee, O God. My soul thirsteth for God, for the living God . . ." (vv. 1-2, KJV).

And the same people to whom Isaiah spoke were speaking for themselves in Psalm 137. They felt wasted in their long captivity in Babylon:

"By the rivers of Babylon, there we sat down, yea, we wept, when we remembered Zion. We hanged our harps upon the willows in the midst thereof. For there they that carried us away captive required of us a song; and they that wasted us required of us mirth, saying, Sing us one of the songs of Zion. How shall we sing the Lord's song in a strange land?" (Psalm 137:1-4, KJV).

Well, moral fatigue is the feeling that we are in a strange land from day to day, week after week, for years on end. Nothing seems to matter much.

Ezekiel went among these people also and his report was the same. While he dwelt among them, he had a vision. And in the vision, he heard them say, "Our bones are dried up, and our hope is lost; we are clean cut off . . ." (Ezekiel 37:11, RSV). This is moral fatigue. It is weariness of the inner man, and it corrodes moral strength.

Even Paul found the task of keeping morally strong to be not an easy one. He had his moments too. In Romans 7:18-24 he tells of his own moral fatigue: "For I know that nothing good dwells within me . . . I can will what is right, but I cannot do it. For I do not do the good I want, but the evil I do not want is what I do" (RSV).

I had a good friend who shot himself to death on Easter Sunday morning. He had been a fervent supporter of every good cause, a good husband, a caring father, and a man of principle. But he had made some bad investments; he had stretched himself too far; his pride was about to be lost, and his courage failed him. Moral fatigue. Suicide.

But the prophet says that there is another answer. God never gets tired and does not faint, ever! "They who wait for the Lord shall renew their strength, they shall mount up with wings like eagles, they shall run and not be weary, they shall walk and not faint."

In order to pull out of this fatigue, begin by taking on small tasks first equal to your strength, until your strength grows. And it will! Start with small victories and pile them up. A friend had a stroke and had temporary paralysis in his right leg. A physical therapist working with him had a rough time getting him to cooperate. He wanted to move his whole leg, right then. She said, "No. Let's start with the big toe. Move it. Get control of that first. Then the whole foot. Then the calf. Then the thigh. One bone at a time." Remember, Ezekiel's vision was converted into a black spiritual that said that those dry bones did not suddenly leap together. The singers remind you that the toe bone connected to the foot bone, the foot bone to the ankle bone, the ankle bone to the leg bone, leg bone to the thigh bone, etc. "Hear the word of the Lord!"

You are responsible for your own opportunity. Nothing more. So use what you have, gain the ground you can, and God will add to your effort. Jesus told the parable of the talents to show us that one-talent servants are under as heavy an obligation as ten-talent ones to do the best they can with what is available to them.

I recall how I quit smoking, many years ago. I began smoking in college. Everybody smoked, it seemed. It was a sign of manhood. So I learned too. Thirty years later I found out how dangerous it was and how it shortened life, with pain. But I loved my Winstons. I was no ordinary Winston smoker. Before lighting up, I smelled each and tapped each end to tighten up the tobacco and let the match burn down to the paper (I never insulted a Winston with a lighter!). But one New Year's Day I promised my younger son, age eight, that I would give him the whole day and do his bidding—only no money and no leaving the house. He agreed.

First he ordered the upstairs, old black-and-white TV downstairs to view two bowl games simultaneously. Next he ordered, "No smoking all day!" *That,* after thirty years of Camels, Kents, L & M's, and tasty Winstons. But he was dead *(sic)* right. And I took him on. I set my clock for 9:00 A.M. I smoked nothing until I heard the bang-a-lang at 9:00. Then I still did not smoke, but I set it for 10:00 A.M. Bang-a-lang! One more hour. I ate every crumb I saw, drank everything that flowed, and nearly climbed the wall, but I lived from one bang-a-lang to another until 10:00 P.M. when I jumped in bed. After thirty years of smoking, I had finally made a full day without, and I have not gone back—yet. Six years now! All this says is that you may not leap from moral fatigue to St. Francis of Assisi or Wilberforce or Frederick Douglass. You may have to pass through some unimpressive stages, growing from "one degree of grace to another," one bang-a-bang at a time.

Next, hold on to those old and well-established principles of morality that have stood the test of time. You may not be living up to them, but keep reaffirming that they belong to you. It is one thing to be lost. It is another to lose your map too! It is one thing to be off course but far worse to have a broken compass. So, however far you may have strayed, keep your principles together.

Our society flounders terribly, for example, on the whole business of welfare, open admissions, a better chance for blacks, Chicanos, and native Americans. Bright people put their racial and tribal interests out front and say the silliest things; they talk as though slavery never happened and the slaughter of Indians was a watermelon feast or a fish fry. They act as though today's disparities have no origins and today's problems have no antecedents. Their principles are lost or hidden.

John Rawls, the Harvard philosopher, has written an extremely helpful book called *A Theory of Justice*. In it he argues that fairness requires us to go further than to give to everyone an equal opportunity. It requires us to look at the starting points that various persons and groups have had and to see how it was that at the *original position* we have very *unequal* beginnings. And we should presume an absolutely equal original position, in order to be fair, and then adjust opportunities and benefits accordingly. We can never correct all the damage done by slavery for 250 years, but we can try.

Everyone knows that. No parent would treat a weak child with a serious cardiac problem the same way one treats a child who has enjoyed perfect health. And no society should be begrudging in helping those handicapped by chronic poverty, poor schools, poor nutrition, and racism to overcome their deficits, to compensate for losses inflicted upon them, and to have a chance to participate fully and fairly in this society.

When I was a boy, we (black people) were barred from the city park except on special days and were denied use of the central library. Every street car, every bus, every theater, every restaurant, and every beach were segregated, and black folk had only menial jobs. I could not apply to the Navy except as a mess boy. Does anyone need to wonder why many blacks, after that kind of treatment for one hundred years, would do poorly on the graduate record examination? But the sad fact is that there are deans and professors who do.

If one is to recover from moral fatigue, one must hold onto the loftiest ideas people have thought, cling to those monumental principles of justice and fairness that have stood the test of time. These principles will bring you through. Go back and hear Moses from Sinai, Amos from Tekoa, John the Baptist from the banks of the Jordan, and Jesus from the Mount of Olives.

Finally, take the quick opener. Be ready to seize upon the first chance at moral greatness you see. Life keeps a parade of opportunities for goodness moving before us, people who need love, causes that need support, services begging for a volunteer. Don't wait for the very one you had in mind. Flex those moral muscles. Move out at the first flash of insight.

A friend of mine is now pastor of the Protestant, ecumenical parish for Americans in Paris. One Sunday morning from his pulpit he saw a black family present with a small blind girl. They turned out to be refugees from an African state that was in political upheaval, homeless and friendless, in Paris, political exiles. After several conversations and many nights of wrestling, my friend, a tall, white, athletic-looking, fast-walking Yankee preacher, ended up with this little, blind, black girl by the hand, on the way to a New York ophthalmologist for the removal of tumors of the cornea.

His full vacation was spent in trips to the doctor's office and to the hospital. I can hear the comments: "Look at that liberal show-off with that poor black child!" Or, "What a helluva job to have carrying a little black girl around!" Or, "I wonder if he married a black woman and if that is his daughter." Anything but a decent man doing a decent thing. Hardly anyone would know that he spotted her from the pulpit, saw her need, and knew how to get help. He only needed the strength to offset *moral fatigue*. And that strength came. Have mercy!

> They who wait for the Lord shall renew their strength,
>   they shall mount up with wings like eagles,
> they shall run and not be weary,
>   they shall walk and not faint.
>   —Isaiah 40:31 (RSV)

A Whole Man
Made Well

John 7:23

Frank Stagg

Salvation may be understood from various perspectives. It is *direction* for one who has lost the way. It is *reconciliation* for one who has been alienated from God, from others, and from oneself. It is *forgiveness* for one who knows oneself to be guilty. It is *cleansing* for one who has been defiled. It is *liberation* for one who has been bound within by guilt, fear, greed, lust, envy, jealousy, prejudice, hate, or whatever, or who has been bound from without by some imposed creed, cultic pattern, or whatever. It is *strength* for one who has found

Frank Stagg, a native of Eunice, Louisiana, is James Buchanan Harrison Professor of New Testament at the Southern Baptist Theological Seminary in Louisville, Kentucky. He is a graduate of Louisiana College and received his Th.M. and Ph.D. degrees from the Southern Baptist Theological Seminary and has done advanced study at other schools including the University of Tübingen, Germany. He has served as pastor of the First Baptist Church in DeRidden, Louisiana, and for twenty years was professor of New Testament and Greek at the New Orleans Baptist Theological Seminary. He was one of the consulting editors for *The Broadman Bible Commentary* and wrote the commentaries on "Matthew" and "Philippians" in this series. Among his many books are *The Book of Acts, New Testament Theology, Polarities of Man's Existence in Biblical Perspective,* and *The Holy Spirit Today.* Louisiana College conferred an honorary LL.D. degree upon him in 1955.

oneself unequal to the demands of life. It is *meaning* for one who has known no real answer to life's recurrent question, Why? In the perspective of John 7:23, salvation is wholeness. It is God's work of making a total person sound.

Properly defined, salvation is God's work of enabling anyone of us to become an authentic human being—no more, no less, and no other than a human being. Salvation is God's achievement in redemption of his intention in creation. Salvation is not becoming divine. Adam, in effect, tried to be God, and thus he became less than human. Whatever may be said for angels, they do not represent a valid goal for human beings. Salvation is not becoming an angel, now or in heaven. Salvation is not by any form of reduction. It is not becoming a mere body or a mere soul. It is not becoming a fraction or a part, whatever the part may be. Salvation is not escape from others, some "lone ranger" or "island" kind of existence. Salvation is not absorption into the "all," the loss of individual identity. Salvation is God's work of enabling one to become a full person. We were made to be, but to be, we must become. Salvation is becoming a true human being, a full person in the presence of God, in the presence of other people, in the presence of the things about us, and in the presence of one's self.

A Cripple Healed

Jesus brought all of this into focus in a far-reaching question, addressed to the piety of his day: "Are you angry with me because on the sabbath day I made a whole man well?" (John 7:23). The question emerges from the story of a healing miracle, bringing into sharp focus the clash between two radically different approaches in religion, one person-centered and the other cultic-centered. To see the point, we must turn to the story begun in chapter 5 and resumed in chapter 7 of John's Gospel.

At one of the gates to the temple in Jerusalem there was a pool whose waters were thought to have a healing quality. Many people gathered there in the hope of being healed. Jesus came upon this scene one day, and he fixed his attention on one man in particular, a man who for thirty-eight years had been lame. Jesus asked the man, "Do you wish to become well [*hygies*]?" That may strike one as a strange way of addressing a lame man. Would not any lame man want to be well? Had not this man come to the pool in the hope of being healed? Was the question superfluous? Not necessarily so. The question was a proper one. Not all really want to be well. There are some advantages to being sick or crippled. There are responsibilities thus escaped. There may be attention enjoyed in illness and not otherwise gained. Health or wholeness does have its demands.

Then, too, it belongs to the nature of personhood that it be free and that wholeness be something accepted and not imposed. Authentic personhood cannot be coerced. One can fix a watch or a motor without the knowledge or consent of the object to be repaired. Given the expertise and equipment for it, a mechanic can compel a motor to run, but no significant fulfillment can be imposed upon a human being. That is why salvation is not just a matter of God's goodwill or love. It is not simply a matter of God so loving that he cannot let us be lost. Precisely because God does love us are we able to be lost. It is because he loves us and because he opens to us the possibility of salvation that he also allows us to self-destruct. God does not will that any person be lost, but because he loves us, we can be lost. This is what is meant by "the wrath of God" as set forth in Romans 1:18-32, the only place in the Bible where "the wrath of God" is the explicit subject developed *in extenso*. Three times Paul declares of those who *chose* not to have God in their knowledge (1:22) that "God gave them up" (1:24, 26, 28). Gave them up to what or to whom? He gave them up to themselves, to their own choices. God gives us the freedom to self-destruct. Only in such freedom do we have the option of becoming truly human. The possibility of being lost is the necessary and calculated risk in all personal existence. It is not because God wills that any be lost but that he wills the freedom of salvation. God does not withdraw from us the freedom he gives, even though we use it to self-destruct. G. B. Caird, commenting on Revelation 20:10, puts it well, "The lake of fire stands at the end of the world's story as a proof of the dignity of man, whom God will never reduce to the status of puppet by robbing him of his freedom of choice."[1]

The "Achilles heel" of "predestination," besides its monstrous and fallacious view of God as arbitrary, is that what it offers as "salvation" is really destruction. Were God to determine that some be "saved" and some be "lost," there would be no meaningful difference between the two groups or fates. Both groups would be lost. Meaning would be denied to both, for freedom would be denied to both. Both would be reduced to the status of things, objects manipulated. Salvation is not salvation for a person unless personhood itself be preserved. That is why Jesus asked the cripple, "Do you wish to become well?"

The lame man was twice crippled and twice healed. Jesus healed the crippled man at two levels of his being: outwardly and within. The lame man was crippled outwardly, unable to walk. He was crippled within, crippled by sin. Jesus first healed the man outwardly, for it was this lameness with which the man was first concerned. Jesus began with what was the man's lesser hurt, for that was the hurt of which the lame man was most aware. Jesus followed no stereotype in ministering to people. He just as well could have begun with the problem within had that been the opening given him by the man's own self-awareness. Jesus gave this man such physical strength that he was able to walk. Later, finding the man in the temple, Jesus commanded him no longer to continue to sin, lest a worse fate befall him (5:14). He thus healed him within, extending his saving work of making a whole man sound.

Sharp criticism came from some of the Jews because it was on the sabbath that Jesus healed the lame man. The healing miracle recorded in chapter 5 of John's Gospel so rankled in the hearts of certain men of piety that the story resurfaces in chapter 7, with focus on the sabbath. The sabbath had become a basic test for Jewish piety in the time of Jesus. If one thinks that the New Testament exaggerates this, read from the Mishnah tractates *Shabbath* and *Erubin,* thirty-six pages in English translation detailing rabbinical regulations for sabbath observance.[2] Rabbinical decisions had worked out every conceivable problem in the interest of a careful observance of the sabbath. The Pharisees had rulings about such matters as the maximum distance that could be walked on the sabbath, how much weight could be lifted, what could be done about a lamp left burning from the day before the sabbath, and the culpability of writing together two letters of the alphabet on the sabbath. The Qumran community, presumably Essene, seems to have been even stricter.[3] This piety is not to be written off as sham or hypocrisy. To the contrary, such was Jewish devotion to this religious understanding that many yielded up their lives to their enemies, preferring to be killed rather than fight on the sabbath. But however sincere, this understanding of piety seems to us to be woefully lacking. It raised to ultimate worth what in itself was thing-centered rather than person-centered. This expression of piety was arbitrary and superficial. It did not arise out of human nature nor necessarily minister to a person's need or fulfillment. Although such practice acquired a certain meaning for those conditioned to it, it was arbitrary, artificial, and superficial. It is not inherent to human nature or need. It is dispensable.

Jesus clashed at many points with the piety of his day, but nowhere was the conflict in perspectives sharper than here. In the lame man at the pool Jesus saw a person; his opponents saw encroachment upon a cultic day. Jesus gave priority to a man in need. His opponents gave priority to a cultic practice. Jesus placed a man above the sabbath (cf. Mark 2:27). His opponents placed the sabbath above a man. However, Jesus stood his ground against an offended piety: "Are you angry with me because on the sabbath I made a whole man well?"

SALVATION AS SOUNDNESS

There is a play on words in the Greek text of John 7:23, difficult to carry over into English. Two Greek words, *holon* and *hygīe*, may both be rendered "whole," but with different connotations. The first of the two words is precisely our word "whole," taken over directly from Greek. This is whole in the sense of total or entire. Jesus had healed the crippled man both outwardly and within, crippled legs as well as his crippling within by sin. The other Greek word is *hygīe*, from which we get the English word "hygienic." This is a word for wholeness as health or soundness. Jesus made the lame man "hygienic" outwardly and inwardly. This is salvation. Salvation is God's work of making a total person well.

Salvation is both a condition and a relationship, the former growing out of the latter. This may be illustrated by contemporary medical practice (the analogy holds for the responsible client, not for the infant or patient incapacitated for responsible decision). It is a physician's business to resist all that leads to sickness and death and, on the positive side, to improve health and extend life. The physician effects this through medicine, programs of diet, balance between rest and exercise, and sometimes surgery. But a physician does not impose this service upon a patient. He or she awaits the client's acceptance of the services. Relationship between physician and client, a relationship of mutual trust, of mutual acceptance and commitment, is the precondition to therapy. But once the relationship is established, therapy begins. That is the whole point in the relationship. So in salvation, there must first be a new relationship of trust, of acceptance and commitment, and then there follows the new quality of life.

Salvation is a new kind of existence, the source of which is in God himself (see 1 John 1:1-3). This means that salvation depends upon a new relationship with God. Jesus once put it this way: "This is eternal life, that they may know thee the only true God, and Jesus Christ whom thou hast sent" (John 17:3, RSV). Salvation is eternal life. Eternal life is that quality of life which derives from God. It is that kind of existence which results when one comes to live under the kingdom of God. The kingdom of God is the rule of God. It means that God is king. To enter the kingdom of God is to accept willingly God's sovereign rule. Under that rule a new kind of life begins.

We have seen already that saving a person is not like saving a thing. Things may be put into order by force. A person at the deepest level of existence cannot be made well except through his or her own consent. We can force Pablum down a baby's throat and give diphtheria shots to the infant, even though the shot is received with kicking and squalling; but no parent, physician, or preacher can force moral, ethical, or other personal qualities upon another person. That is why Jesus began by asking the lame man, "Do you wish to become well?" Jesus was interested in more than strong legs. That is why faith is absolutely indispensable to salvation. Saving faith is trust, openness to God. It is the trust which is openness to receive what God offers and to yield what he demands. Saving faith is not to be confused with creedalism. Good doctrine has importance, but one is not saved by believing this or that, no matter what this or that may be. One is saved by the Savior, not by this or that or by believing this or that. One is saved only as the living Christ becomes in one a living and transforming presence. Christ thus enters through the door of faith, as one trusts enough to be open to his presence.

Salvation, then, is a relationship and a condition. The condition of soundness grows out of the personal relationship of faith. This soundness looks toward complete soundness. Of course, none of us is completely sound. Perfection belongs to God and to him alone. But the goal of being totally sound is the goal in salvation. Nothing short of a whole person made "hygienic" is a proper goal under the lordship of Christ.

BEING AND BECOMING

In writing to the Corinthians, Paul spoke of "those who are

perishing" and those "who are being saved" (1 Corinthians 1:18). He saw each as a process, one moving toward ruin and the other moving toward the fullness of salvation. Indeed, salvation is seen in the New Testament in three dimensions: past, present, and future. Paul could look back to his Damascus Road experience as the beginning of his salvation. He also could declare that salvation was nearer for his readers than when they first believed (Romans 13:11). He referred here to the consummation of salvation in the resurrection beyond this life. But Paul also saw salvation as a process, as something dynamic and moving, not static and fixed. The lost are oriented toward death, moving away from true selfhood. Those being saved are oriented toward life, moving in the direction of fulfillment. The goal is yet ahead, and the goal is completion in Christ. It is that the whole man may ultimately be well.

ARE YOU SAVED?

It is not uncommon to hear one ask, "Are you saved?" "When were you saved?" It is not uncommon for one to say, "I was saved blank years ago." Saved from what? Saved to what? Many who boast that they are saved are obviously yet crippled. Many are neurotic. Many have deep-seated antisocial attitudes and feelings. Some are violent. Many live under the tyranny of fear, calling it phobia. Many are enslaved by greed, lust, pride, prejudice, envy, jealousy, hostility, or even hate. What about being saved to love, joy, peace, patience, kindness, goodness, faith/fidelity, gentleness, and self-control (Galatians 5:22)?

It follows that none is completely free from those feelings, attitudes, and actions which dehumanize us. Forces are at work in all of us which yet tend to enslave, degrade, deplete, and destroy. But if salvation is authentic and meaningful, there are forces at work in the other direction. Salvation is God's work of liberating us. It is forgiveness, cleansing, healing, restoration, direction, and new resources for fulfillment as persons. Salvation is God's work in enabling one to become human. A human being is being human.[4] Salvation is God's work in humanizing those otherwise dehumanized. It is making a whole person sound.

Salvation should be meaningful in terms of personal fulfillment. Apparently much that is called salvation adds little if any meaning to human existence. In part this is because salvation is sometimes presented only in transactional terms, not really penetrating one's existence. It is not a caricature to say some preach salvation thus: Adam blew it and we all bear his guilt; Jesus took the rap for us; the transaction has been written up theologically as "the plan of salvation." If we believe the plan of salvation, we are saved. Nothing of this necessarily penetrates our existence. All of this can remain external and superficial. It has no necessary bearing on the inner self, precisely where Jesus found the essence or origin of good and evil. Salvation is not meaningful unless it affects one's inner world of feeling, attitude, intention, values, principles, and commitment as well as one's relationship with God, with other people, with things, and with oneself.

Whether salvation has meaning or not depends in part on one's understanding of the holistic nature of the person. There are various views, ancient and modern, in which a human being is understood as partitive, consisting of dichotomous, trichotomous, or multichotomous parts: soul and body; soul, spirit, and body; or mind and body. This is not a sound understanding of a human being. One is aspective but not partitive.[5] One is highly complex, with body, mind, feeling, will, reason, aesthetic sense, moral sense, awareness of the transcendent, etc. These are distinguishable aspects of selfhood, but they are not separable parts. One cannot extract feeling or will or reason from one another. There is thought only as a person thinks; and as one thinks, one also feels or wills. There is will only as one wills, and one does not will without also feeling and thinking. We are holistic, and we are highly aspective. Meaningful salvation gives coherence to a holistic self, and it affects one in every aspect of one's personhood: reason, feeling, will, body, and all else. This is Christ's work of making a whole person sound.

Meaningful salvation affects one in one's individual identity, and it affects one in relationship with others. Individual identity is an essential without which one has no meaningful existence. You are you and no one else; no one else is you. Mary dare not yield to Martha's demand that she become Martha; and Martha has no right to require that Mary become Martha (Luke 10:38-42). God remains the God of Abraham, Isaac, and Jacob. Isaac is Isaac, not Abraham or Jacob. So with each. In creation or birth and in redemption individual selfhood is to be preserved and heightened. But that is not all. The other side of the polarity is relationship with others. No one is an island. No one lives or dies to oneself. One cannot *be* alone. Authentic selfhood can emerge only in relationship with God and other people. Meaningful salvation is a possibility only in the polarity of individual identity and community, each real and neither sacrificed to the other.

Meaningful salvation requires that justice be done to one's dual kinship to God and to creation, or to God and the earth. We are created in the image of God. This is the basic polarity of human existence. We are created, thus creatures. We belong to creation. We are made from the ground or earth. We are creatures, but we are more. We are made in the image of God, but we are not God. Our polar identity is unique. Much of our failure is in the neglect of one polar dimension or the other. We sometimes rebel against our creaturehood and try to be God. This is idolatry and ruin. Sometimes we rebel against our divine kinship and try to be mere creatures. This is materialism or secularism. Adam was tempted to be God, and he became less than human. Sometimes we try to sink down into our creaturehood and be mere animals or creatures. To reject either polar claim is to be lost. Meaningful salvation is making the whole person sound: creature yet more, like God yet not God.

Do you wish to be well? You may become so. You will not be compelled to become well. God and other people have much to do with the options before you, but in the final analysis you exercise the option. If willing, you may become a whole person made sound. There is meaning for you. There is meaning proportionate to your faith or openness to God, to others, to the world about you, and to your own full potential.

Trying to
Walk on Water

Matthew 14:22-33; Mark 6:45-51

G. Avery Lee

One afternoon at the hospital I was drinking coffee with one of
the chaplain interns, Mark Gasquet, an Episcopal minister. Mark is
recently out of the military chaplaincy. He told of a fellow
Episcopalian who was Chief of Chaplains of the United States Army,
with the rank of Major General. The Chief had retired and become a
local parish priest in a small place. As Mark Gasquet put it: "The
General went from walking on the water to St. Swithin's-by-the-
Ghetto, where he could barely stay afloat."

G. Avery Lee is pastor of St. Charles Avenue Baptist Church,
New Orleans, Louisiana. He is a native of Oklahoma City,
Oklahoma, and a graduate of Hardin-Simmons University and
Yale University Divinity School. In addition to serving as pastor in
Connecticut, Illinois, and Texas, he has served as Director of
Baptist Student Work at Louisiana State University. He has been
on various denominational boards and committees including
serving as Chairman of the Christian Life Commission of the
Southern Baptist Commission, the Executive Board of the
Louisiana Baptist Convention, and Past President of the Greater
New Orleans Federation of Churches. He has written many
varieties of denominational materials and is the author of seven
books including *What's Right with the Church, Roads to God,
The Reputation of a Church,* and *I Want That Mountain.* Hardin-
Simmons University has conferred upon him the honorary
Doctor of Literature degree.

There is something in Mark's story of the general whose every whim was taken care of to the parish priest who had to struggle. He was the same man, but the circumstances were different. I don't think either walking on water or struggling to stay afloat had anything to do with the man's faith, either the quality or the quantity of his faith, that is. Different circumstances called for a different variety of faith.

Matthew, Mark, and John recorded the episode of Jesus' walking on the water. Luke left it out. Parallels to the story are found in Hellenistic literature, and there is an incident as far back as the life of Buddha. There are some variations in the way Matthew and Mark relate the incident. For example, Mark says nothing about Peter's attempt to walk on the water. Why he left that out, who knows? His probable reason is because the point of the story in Mark is not to display supernatural power—Mark seldom does that. In Mark, the story is simply an account of Jesus' concern for his disciples who were in danger.

Both Matthew and Mark have the incident coming immediately after the feeding of the five thousand with five loaves and two fish. John also records the event in the same sequence. Matthew and Mark have Jesus telling the disciples to get in the boat and start on ahead of him while he dismissed the crowd and went off to pray. John says Jesus thought "they were about to take him and force him to be king," and he went off into the hills by himself, with no instructions for the disciples. Matthew doesn't even say where they were going. Mark has Jesus sending them to Bethsaida at the north end of the sea. But we don't know where they started from. John has them going to Capernaum. In all three cases a storm came up. They were hard-pressed, rowing against the wind and waves.

All three accounts have Jesus walking *on* the sea. However, a good linguistic case can be made for walking *by* the sea. But, let's not get technical about the use of a word. For our purposes, let's use the word "on."

Jesus was off alone, praying. Only Mark says that Jesus was aware of the trouble the disciples were in:

> He saw that they were making headway painfully, for the wind was against them (6:48, RSV).

Mark also has a strange sentence, not used by Matthew or John:

> . . . he came to them, walking on the sea. *He meant to pass by them* (italics added).

Or, as the King James Version puts it:

He would have passed them by.

Now, why would Mark have Jesus do a thing like that? If he was going to the rescue, why pass by them?

Again, perhaps it was Mark's intention to tell an eloquent story of human distress. The storm did not come when the disciples had embarked on some foolish enterprise of their own. They were doing what Jesus told them to do! The storms of life come, sometimes, even when we are doing what we should. You see, following Jesus does not mean that we are immune from trouble or that we escape stormy weather. Nor does doing right mean that life will be easy. Sometimes doing right gets us into all kinds of trouble.

This is perhaps an unintended but true picture of prayer at its best. Jesus was alone in prayer. That doesn't mean he was on his knees with his eyes closed. He was alone in those hills but was aware of what was going on. Can we picture him sitting there, quietly thinking and praying, but also with his eyes open, alert to what was happening?

Prayer is not an exercise in a vacuum. While there was the upward reach to God, there was also the outward reach to others. People were not absent from Jesus' mind even when he was praying. What about us? Is it not easier for us to pray for people starving in Africa than it is to send some relief money? Or is it easier to pray for people in the inner city than it is to give some time to one of our mission centers? When prayer is truly Christian, it is not enclosed in the walls of some personal petition. True prayer changes from petition to intercession to action.

Perhaps it was a moonlit night, and Jesus could see the sea, even though it was cloudy. Seeing the waves and feeling the wind, he was alerted to the disciples' needs. Ah, those contrary winds, when life heads into a gale! Waves too heavy for our strength to pull against roll up, and we are distressed in rowing. Then Jesus comes.

"When they saw him walking on the sea they thought it was a ghost, and cried out; for they all saw him, and were terrified. But immediately he spoke to them and said, 'Take heart, it is I; have no fear'" (Mark 6:49-50, RSV).

This is a vivid drama of one of Jesus' central teachings: God's knowledge of his children and his care for them. There is sheer eloquence in the words "he came." Into unnumbered lives, including yours and mine, distressed with life's storms, engulfed by the waves, and buffeted by the winds so that rowing is hard, he has come. That is history. That is fact. That is the Christian's personal experience. He has come with the assurance of God's care. Into homes of grief, lives of discouragement, failure, and anguish, he has come, just as he did that night in Galilee.

The verb "to come" has present and future tense as well as past. Jesus *came* to the disciples in their distress.

He *has come* to others in desperate hours.

He *comes* to us in the present.

But there is the future *he will come,* and that gives us confidence.

Only Matthew records the incident of Peter's effort to join Jesus in the walk:

> "Lord, if it is you, bid me come to you on the water." He said, "Come." So Peter got out of the boat and walked on the water and came to Jesus; but when he saw the wind, he was afraid, and beginning to sink he cried out, "Lord, save me." Jesus immediately reached out his hand and caught him, saying to him, "O man of little faith, why did you doubt?" And when they got in the boat, the wind ceased (14:28-32).

Peter is characteristically impulsive. He leaps before he looks. Well, that is better than to look so long that one never leaps at all, as some among us do. Peter is mixed in motives. But aren't we all! He genuinely wants to be with Jesus, but maybe he wants to show that he could do what Jesus was doing.

"Look, fellas, I'm walking on the water!"

He begins well, as many do; but when he saw the storms, he was afraid, as many of us are. Peter was helpless, as every person is, without God.

Why did his faith fail? Maybe because, when his venture began, he had his eyes partly on Jesus and partly on himself. Maybe because, as the venture continued, he looked at the storm more than at Jesus.

"When he saw the wind, he was afraid."

That, too, is like many of us.

In the old days of sailing vessels, when a new sailor climbed the narrow rope ladder to the crow's nest, the old hands would shout: "Look up! Look up!" If the climber looked down, he might get dizzy and fall. Faith keeps its eyes fixed on God. But Peter's eyes wavered.

"O man of little faith, why did you doubt?"

But Jesus never fails us, even if we have but half faith.

"Jesus immediately reached out his hand and caught him."

Trust in God, in Jesus Christ, is never misplaced. On a later occasion when Jesus asked Peter if he loved him, he never did get the full answer he wanted. But Jesus took what love Peter did offer and used that. My, how he used it!

There is the question: Just what is enough faith? As a grain of mustard seed? Enough to move a mountain? Well, I think that varies from person to person, from time to time, from event to event. Rather than for any of us to say that some other of us has too little faith, why not be thankful for what little faith one of us might have?

One reason why some folk find themselves in difficulty with Christian faith is that their expectations concerning the Christian life have been very high, but in their experiences of it they have been disappointed. There are those storms that come when we're doing what we're told, for example. The problem is not theoretical doubt, but practical disillusionment. Why should the Christian suffer the same outraged fortune as the non-Christian? The difficulty lies in the expectation that the Christian life, while it may be theoretically true, is not practically what some advertise it to be. It is not an escape from all of life's storms; it is a way to weather those storms.

There are those who expect from the Christian experience a life of joy and quietude, which they have not found. They are led to expect this by those passages of Scripture which speak about "the peace that passes understanding." They are bothered by the testimonies of some Christians who speak about living without ever experiencing depressed hours or flagging spirits.

Why is it that Christians are loathe to speak about their frustrations, doubts, or trouble with sin? Probably because we think people *expect* us to say only the good, positive things, because we think people expect us as Christians never to be bothered with such things.

Of course, there are times of high emotional joy and deep inner peace. But we must not demand that as a condition for keeping our faith. We ought not to seek God simply for the sake of sensational experiences, no matter how desirable they may be.

There are some who come into the Christian life because they need some conquering power in their struggle against sin. They are told that absolute victory can be theirs through faith in Jesus Christ. And they set their hopes on that. But they are disappointed. That they have been helped they would not deny. But they find that the battle with besetting sin is a running fight; it has not been concluded in a final, resounding victory. This seems to be a denial of what some preachers have promised. And it is. Preachers are not infallible. And some Christians take a holy stance and remind them of their weakness.

No one is ever so totally freed from sin that one never sins again. One *is* forgiven, and in Jesus Christ one has an ally in the struggle. Faith in the forgiving love of God in Christ becomes a resource, not a talisman.

I read of a great preacher who all his life had to do battle with alcohol, which had once mastered him. His fight never ceased. His victory of faith consisted not in the elimination of the problem, but in his constant struggle with it and his refusal of subjugation to it. Perhaps an equally strong ally was his congregation who admired and loved him all the more because he was honest with them. They saw him struggle. They saw his steadfast will, sustained by his faith. And they believed in him. But it takes an unusual group of Christian people to share that much honesty—to allow for human frailty, not demanding that their pastor *walk on water,* but allowing him to walk *by* the sea with them.

To walk on water requires faith. To walk *by* the water requires faith, too. "Now faith means we are confident of what we hope for, convinced of what we do not see" (Hebrews 11:1, Moffatt).

We cannot live without faith, because we deal not only with a past which we may know and a present which we can see, but also with *a future in whose possibilities we must believe.* We can no more avoid looking ahead when we live our lives than we can when we sail a boat. In one case as in the other, our direction is determined by our thought of what lies ahead of us, our "confidence of what we hope for." This future into which we continually press our way can never be a matter of demonstrable knowledge. We know only when we arrive. But in the meantime we believe. Our knowledge of what is and what has been is not more necessary than our faith concerning what is to come.

Remember, Peter had not yet given his classic confession of faith concerning Jesus, "You are the Christ, the Son of the living God." Nor had Peter had the experience of the Mount of Transfiguration.

Peter had a lot of "future faith" in possibilities he did not know about.

We cannot live without faith, because our relationship with the future is an affair not of thought alone but of action. Life is a continuous adventure into the unknown. Abraham and Moses pushing out into experiences whose outcome they could not see are typical of lives that have adventured for God. So Peter's stepping onto the water was an adventure into the unknown. Awkward as that step was, he took it. By faith everyone of us must undertake each plain day's work if we are to do it well, *or at all.*

Before we talk about Peter's lack of faith, let's give him credit for the right action of starting toward Jesus with what little faith he did have. That's what mattered. And, remember, Jesus reached out and took him in—back into the boat.

To Live
Is to Love

1 John 4:7-21

Paul D. Simmons

Love is the predominant theme in the Johannine literature. Both the Gospel and the letters of John bear this indelible characteristic. Everywhere and at each point in John's declarations about God and his analysis of the Christian life, love is the basic criterion and the final consideration. One cannot speak of God unless one speaks of love, for "God is love." One cannot understand the Christian life unless one knows the demands of love. This perspective permeates each page and punctuates every affirmation as John portrays the love

Paul D. Simmons, a native of Tennessee, is presently Associate Professor of Christian Ethics at the Southern Baptist Theological Seminary in Louisville, Kentucky. He is a graduate of Union University and received his B.D. and Th.M. degrees from Southeastern Baptist Theological Seminary in Wake Forest, North Carolina, and his Ph.D. from Southern Baptist Theological Seminary. Before beginning his teaching career, he served as pastor in Tennessee and North Carolina. Noted as a popular conference and lecture speaker, he has spoken before many college, church, and ministerial associations. He is listed in *Who's Who in Religion, Directory of American Scholars,* and *Dictionary of International Biographies.* He is coauthor of *Growing Up with Sex,* has contributed seven articles in *Baker's Dictionary of Christian Ethics,* and has written for numerous other scholarly and denominational publications.

of God as the basis for our lives. For John, the meaning of life is to be discovered in love—the love of God as revealed to us in Christ. In a very real sense, John's thesis is "To Live Is to Love."

My initial reaction to this notion was highly negative, however. I had been asked to speak on this topic at a student convention. I remember thinking that the whole idea was incredible. My cynical smile betrayed the feeling that "to live is *not* to love. Look what loving got Jesus—a cross! If one wants to go on living, one had better *not* be loving." Certainly, the cross of Christ warns of the dangerous pilgrimage on "the road of the loving heart."

The idea also seemed incredible because there are so many people alive who are not loving. Too many people are "beasts misnamed men" who carry out acts of violence and cruelty. They live even though they hate. There is nothing automatic in the relation between living and loving. One may live and not love. One may love and not live. Certainly one does not live as long as one loves, else we would all live as long as we had someone to love. Too many live who do not love. Too many die even though they love.

Another reaction I felt against this idea was "that's not necessarily true!" It all depends on what you mean by "love" and "life." The sensualist would strongly agree that "to live is to (make) love." That person's response to the theme would be "Right on! I'm really living when I'm making love." The trail of broken hearts and dreams left by the sensualist's version of love is tragic testimony of some person's confusion between love and lust. One rock singer screams into the microphone that "Without love, life is nothing." He has the right idea, but one suspects the wrong notion of love. A great deal is packaged and passed off as love that does not give evidence of right living. The sensualist's version of love is egocentric and exploitative. This love is the self seeking its own satisfaction, not the good of the beloved. Living like this cannot be loving.

Finally, the recognition dawned on me that John was challenging precisely these notions. He took pains to spell out his meanings and to correct popular misunderstandings. He was careful to illustrate his truth and portray the models by which he thought of love. He was calling for a new way of looking at the relationship between love and life. For him, both "life" and "love" could be understood only in the light of the life and love of Jesus Christ.

John's first affirmation was that *genuine living cannot be separated from love:* "In this the love of God was made manifest among us, that God sent his only Son into the world, so that we might live through him" (1 John 4:9, RSV) For John, we have no life apart from the love of God. Our lives have no meaning apart from the love of God.

There is a difference between living and being alive, of course. We all know this from experience—our own or that of someone near to us. Two words for "life" are used in the New Testament: *bios* and *zoa*. *Bios* is biological functioning—some people call that "life." The term here is *zoa*, the life that God gives—John usually links it to *aionios*—"eternal." The life that God gives is more than biological functioning; it is "of eternity." It has quality, not just function.

There are times when "life" seems more like death. Doctors say that someone is "alive." Machines detect waves from her brain though she cannot speak or breathe on her own. Her life is imprisoned in a coma. Even her body retreats from the doctor's definition of life. Her living is more death than life.

The existentialists spoke of "the living dead." They sensed John's truth that life must be more than *bios*. They saw persons who had never "come alive." Though they were persons, they were not really alive. One woman suffering from depression cried out to her counselor, "I just feel dead!" Her feelings were numb. There was no living left, just life. She had lost love, and life seemed hollow and dead. Robbed of meaning, her living seemed now a dreadful sentence of execution.

Lovers have experienced the point John was making. In finding love, they also find life. Loving puts a spring in one's step and a new joy in existence. Love inspires dreams, enlivens hope, and gives a reason to live. No wonder the poet wrote "not where I breathe, but where I love, I live."

Viktor Frankl, the founder of the school of logotherapy, wrote of his own discovery of this truth in *Man's Search for Meaning*. After describing the wretched existence of life in a concentration camp and the suicidal despair that destroyed so many inmates, Frankl turned to describe the reason for his own survival. One morning, Frankl and other inmates were being taken under heavy guard to their work site. Stumbling in the darkness, with swollen, broken flesh on feet further tortured by huge stones, icy water, and frigid winds, the man next to him humorously said, "If our wives could see us now!" Frankl's mind turned to thoughts of his own wife, now in another camp—dead or alive he did not know. Her image appeared in his mind, and he heard her talking with him, smiling and encouraging him. "A thought," he said, "transfixed me: for the first time in my life I saw the truth. . . . that love is the ultimate and the highest goal to which man can aspire." It was in that moment that Frankl came to see that great secret he had never really understood before: *"The salvation of man is through love and in love."*[1]

That's the truth John was driving home: living is tied to loving. Those who do not know the love of God are "dead"; they have not "come alive." Those who love know what it is to live.

A second affirmation is that *true love is always self-giving:* "the love of God was . . . that he sent his only Son. . . ." For John, all love is tested by the self-giving love of God. We know that "God is love," because he *gave his Son* that all may have life. Divine life is a giving love. Thus, genuine life for a person is a love that gives of itself to and for the beloved.

The distinctive word in the New Testament for this love is *agape.* The meaning of this type of love can only be found in the portrait of the life of Christ. *That* is what it means to love. His love is always self-giving, never self-seeking; Jesus "came not to be served but to serve" (Mark 10:45, RSV). Those who dare to love *like that* must also give themselves: "For whoever would save his life will lose it, and whoever loses his life for my sake will find it" (Matthew 16:25, RSV).

The sensualist never understands this. For such a one, the purpose of life is to get, not to give; it is to seek the good of the self, not the good of the other. Christ's love was a giving of himself for the good of others even to the point of dying that others might live.

Furthermore, such love is not conditional. There is no bargaining of love given for love received: "I will love you *if* you love me in return." In Ingmar Bergman's "Winter Light," Marta loves a disillusioned pastor. Though lacking in faith, he performs the rituals of faith. Bitter and loveless, he is still loved by the patient Marta who follows him on his dreary rounds and attempts to help him back to faith. Though unloved, she loves. One girl, discussing this seeming absurdity in Bergman's play, declared, "But don't we love in order to be loved?"

Not according to John. For him, "we love, because he loved us first" (v. 19). God loved the world, not in order to be loved, but that the world might be saved (John 3:16). Even when a person is unlovely, unloving and loveless, that person is loved by the Father. God's love is unconditional in its self-giving. "Love itself," wrote C. S.

Lewis, "is not a hunger that needs to be filled, but a fullness that gives away."

The point John is making is that it is not in being loved but in loving that our wholeness comes. Only as one is able to give oneself away in love to the other can one claim that one is loving. Real life, then, is not dependent on whether someone finds me to love, but whether I find someone to love. Only a selfish egocentrism permits one to go around asking, "Where is someone to love me?" Love has meaning when it asks: "Where is someone for me to love?"

John's truth for this is drawn from the cross. In his crucifixion, Christ is loving the world, not insisting the world love him. That's why God is revealed so perfectly in the love of Christ: that's the way God loves. His love always gives; the beloved will not always respond. As Paul Scherer has put it: "Love is a spendthrift."[2]

Many Christians active in the civil rights struggle of the sixties failed to grasp this truth. Some, who had worked long hours, marched hundreds of miles in rain, heat, and cold, or lobbied relentlessly in legislative centers, became disillusioned when blacks seemed unappreciative. In spite of legal gains, "whitey" was still regarded with suspicion as "the enemy." When that happened, some complained that blacks should "be grateful for what we have done for them. Don't they see what we've gone through? Why don't they love us?" Some turned from being friendly allies to hostile opponents of blacks seeking further gains against ingrained discrimination. They failed to catch the point of the gospel story: love is patient and persistent even in the face of recalcitrance and loveless rebellion. If love is given *on the condition* it be loved and respected in turn, it is not the love of the cross. For John, genuine loving is always self-giving.

The final affirmation is this: to live is to love; *only as we love do we live.* "God is love," wrote John, "and he who abides in love abides in God, and God abides in him" (v. 16). Only as one participates in God's life of love, does one live, according to John. The ethical imperative is driven home. As God *is* love, so we must be loving. For John, human life is tied to loving. Love is an essential of our very being. Thus, if we are to live, if we are to have "everlasting life," we must love. To fail to love is to die; to love is to live.

This puts a new perspective on the commandment to "love the Lord your God with all your [whole being] . . . and your neighbor as your self" (Matthew 22:37, 39, RSV). The command "to love" is a command to live, to "come alive." The command is: "Love and you will live." The warning is: "Do not love and you will die." The offer of love is the offer of life; to refuse love is to reject life and choose death.

John's model for this is the resurrection of Jesus. Here he introduces an apparent absurdity as the touchstone and foundation for Christian thinking about love and life. The cross seems to say that loving *like that* will bring death. But the resurrection of Christ says that those who love will never die. Christ's resurrection shows that those who love can be killed, but they cannot be destroyed. Thus the irony: to love is to live, otherwise one dies.

One's choices about love are therefore decisions about life and living. Jeremiah stated it strongly: "Behold, I set before you the way of life and the way of death" (Jeremiah 21:8). All about us there are signs that seem to say that "unless we love, we die." Marriage lives only where couples love. Here, in the most intimate of all human relationships love is constantly tested as to its capacity for patience and self-giving. Where there is love, there is life. The partnership lives, and the life of the couple "comes alive" with radiant joy and high emotion.

The races will also either choose life or death. Racial hatred will erupt into a war of bitterness, brother against brother, neighbor against neighbor. But love for neighbor—black for white, white for black—assures life for each, not death for both.

The problem of ecology focuses our love in relation to nature. Hatred in the form of exploitation and pollution is destroying the natural environment. Our home is becoming uninhabitable and hostile. By our use of technology we have chosen not to "love" nature, and thus nature dies and its death spells our doom. To love God's world is to live; otherwise nature dies and with it we die.

War illustrates the relationship of love and life most dramatically, of course. International hostilities begin in the hatreds of economic, territorial, or nationalistic pride. Efficient war machines and arrogant political regimes combine to slaughter millions of the people of the world. Isaiah's dream of a world where people would "beat their swords into plowshares and their spears into pruning hooks" and where "nation shall not lift up sword against nation, neither shall they learn war any more" (Isaiah 2:4) is possible only when people are transformed by the love of God. *Then*—when they learn to love—they will live, and not die by the sword.

Thomas Kepler once described a dramatic experience that happened to him on December 7, 1941, that vividly illustrates these alternatives. Kepler and his wife had been listening to Handel's *Messiah* being broadcast from the Lawrence College Chapel. The music portrayed the way the world ought to live. It spoke of the Messiah and his way of love. Then, Kepler said, a slight turn of the radio dial brought news of the bombings of Pearl Harbor, that resulted in the United States' involvement in World War II. The shift in the dial presented a vivid sign of the alternatives open: the love of the Messiah, or the hatreds and death of war.[3]

Recently, worldwide attention has been focused on the Ik, a tribe in northern Uganda, Africa. This tribe is literally and rapidly going out of existence. The tribe is dying. The people of the tribe live entirely for themselves. Children are put out of the home at the age of three. They are forced to provide food for themselves or die from starvation. One anthropologist who has visited the tribe reported that there is now no one alive who remembers an act of kindness between members of families or of the tribe. Commenting on their return to living by the laws of "raw nature tooth and claw," the anthropologist commented that the people had "lost their humanness." Because they no longer have the capacity to love—to care for one another—they are dying. They are dying physically because they are dead spiritually.

The Ik are a sign for all of us. In a negative way, they illustrate the truth of John's message: to live is to love. Only those who love truly live the life of God.

A Christian Explanation of Your Life

Ephesians 4:11-13

Gardner Taylor

"Ah, Sweet Mystery of Life," is the title of a song we all have sung. The mystery of life, a search for its meaning, if it has any, has occupied men and women through the ages, from the profound scholar to the humblest of us going about our ordinary duties. What does it mean? That is what we keep asking ourselves.

Some say that our lives have no meaning. They are a hodgepodge of this and that, of joy and sorrow. This happens and then that, but, forget it, none of it means anything. A notable line

---

Gardner C. Taylor, a Louisiana native, is pastor of the Concord Baptist Church of Christ in Brooklyn, New York. He is a graduate of Leland College and Oberlin Graduate School of Theology. He has been the preacher for the National Radio Pulpit and many other churches, conventions, and colleges. He has served as a member of the General Council of the American Baptist Convention, Past President of the Progressive National Baptist Convention, Past President of the Protestant Council of Churches of the City of New York, and Past Vice-President of the Urban League of the City of New York. His sermons have been published in such collections as *Best Sermons* (1959), *The Cry of Freedom*, and *Images of Faith.* In 1957, Oberlin College presented him with one of its first alumni citations for his influence as a preacher. He has been honored with three honorary doctor's degrees. In 1973 the Order of the Star of Africa was conferred upon him by President William R. Tolbert, Jr., of the Republic of Liberia.

from one of the noblest men of letters spoke for that point of view in the sentiment, "Life is a tale told by an idiot, full of sound and fury, signifying nothing."

"It is all a matter of fate or fortune," another says. Once in Egypt, at the bazaar in Cairo, a merchant spilled a bottle of fine perfume. Mrs. Taylor and I, startled, expressed pain and sorrow. "It's nothing," the merchant said. "It's for luck." I thought I heard the notion that we should not worry about anything, since everything in life is by chance and our years are one long throw of the dice.

These and other such notions may go down very well for people who are not Christians, and I suppose that they need some disarming explanation of their lives or, better still, some theory which will save them from too strenuous a faith and from looking up too sharply. These explanations of life which I have suggested above will not stand inspection for one moment for Christian people, not for any person who knows that a kind Father and a loving Savior and a sustaining Holy Spirit have been in their lives. Such people can point to various places and times and conditions in which they know that some kind intervention, a gracious intrusion, has occurred on their behalf. They have known a great deliverance which cannot be explained except by the word "God."

Paul is dealing with a Christian explanation of what life is all about in the fourth chapter of his letter to the Ephesians. He comes at the meaning of life for Christians by talking of various phases of work in the church. Admittedly, this chapter deals with the internal affairs of the household of faith, but it will do no violence to the thought of Paul to expand his references to all of life. I say this because, for Christians, their daily work is an extension of their Sunday work, or their church work. The Christian idea of vocation is not that a person shows Christianity solely by what we call church work. Christians show their Christianity by extending into the world and into their daily occupations what they are taught in their church.

Paul speaks of the work of the ministry. Now ministry means not just an ordained pastor or preacher; ministry means serving. Ministry means work in the name of the Lord. We can work for the Lord while we do our daily work. Each Christian is the Lord's man or woman, the Savior's agent, if you please, in his or her sphere of operation. In fact, we need people serving Christ in and during their daily work more than we need more ministers.

Every Christian should look on his or her daily work as an

opportunity to serve Christ in some way or another by honesty, honorableness, and faithfulness in the Lord's service. A television technician was repairing my television set. He lives in White Plains and I had never met him, since I was not at home when he took the set away. Later I talked with him on the telephone. There was something unusual about the way he talked. He was supposed to deliver the television on a certain day. On the day before the delivery date he called to say that he was having car trouble and would have to postpone delivery. There was something honest and open and appealing about the way he spoke. Frankly, I have been so conditioned in the ways of New York business people that I was suspicious. We worked out a way for this technician to bring the television set to the house, and I was there when he came. Quietly he went to work and I sat watching him, fascinated in the way that those of us who have absolutely no talent for mechanics and technology are fascinated by it. Deftly working with his screwdriver, pliers, and wires behind the television, he said to me, "Tell me about the resurrection." We talked. Then he said, as his head disappeared behind the cabinet, "The Lord answers prayers. I have experienced that in my work." What a moving testimony done in daily labor! Here is what we need—people, doing the work of the world, who are Christians and who try in their work, because they are Christians, to make the world a little more like their Lord would have it. Christians should strive to make the lot of those among whom they work a little easier and, as they get opportunity, speak a word for their Lord.

This is the spirit we Christian people must show in our daily work. I was much impressed one evening at the commencement of our church's elementary school. The principal spoke of the chairpersons of our various church boards—Christian people who do or have done daily work. She referred to one of them as a former bakery official and Christian, another a retired transit worker and Christian, another a retired registered nurse and Christian, another a cost accountant and Christian, another a teacher, a reading specialist and Christian. And so on and on. We ought all to think of ourselves as God's people in that way: office worker and Christian, mechanic and Christian, truck driver and Christian, cook and Christian, social worker and Christian. All of us are called on in our work, through it, to make the world a little closer to what our God would have it be, to make it a little nearer to the mind of Christ, a little more responsive to our holy faith.

Someone may be saying to himself: "All well and good for him to be telling us about the importance of our work, but does he know how drab and unexciting I find my work? No one really sees what I try to do and no one cares. People are unpleasant, my feet hurt, and I get nervous and on edge." To such a thought I would have to say that the word "work" may mean all of that. There is a word in our language for "work," and there is a word in our language for "play." They do not mean the same thing. Work is concerned with something that has to get done which requires effort, not just physical effort, mind you, for less and less frequently is any work merely physical effort. All work does mean putting forth effort of some kind. Even those of us who greatly enjoy our work do not like all of it. I do not know of any occupation which does not have its unpleasant, dull side. Yes, there is resistance to getting the job done. There is misunderstanding in work. There is, to be blunt, suffering of some kind in any work we do. There is physical weariness; there is mental exhaustion; there is emotional letdown and uncertainty as to how it is going to come out in any kind of work whatsoever. The work we do, if done in the name of our Lord, is to make the world a little more like what he would have it be. The suffering we encounter while doing our work, if offered to the Lord, can make us what God would have us become. Our work is to make the world better. Our suffering is to make us better.

Now, ask me why this must be and I will have to answer, I do not know—I only know it is so. I know that no athlete ever gets in condition by lolling about; he or she must strain against something, must sweat, get tired. I only know that in the divine economy stress, strain, and suffering, if you please, are necessary to get us to what God would have us. I read of our Lord that "though he were a son, yet learned he obedience by the things he suffered and being made perfect . . ." (Hebrews 5:8, KJV). The passage goes on as if to say that the suffering and the perfection are mixed together.

One sees the relationship between work and suffering in our Lord's experience. He spoke again and again of his work. "Know you not that I must be about my Father's business?" Work, if you please. Listen to him again, "I must work the works of him that sent me." Again, "The Father works hitherto and I work." It was a good work to which he set himself, and if ever a workman should have been warmly received with everything turning out right, it was our Lord. He loved people, but people hated him; he told people the truth, but people lied to him. He helped people, but people set out to hurt him.

The leaders of his nation should have received him, for he was and is the desire of all nations. They would not have him. They should have brought him to his temple in honor. Instead they slew him outside the city's gates.

How did he take it? He was moving in God's will, and so he accepted what happened to him. "The cup which my Father hath given me, shall I not drink of it?" On Calvary he drank the bitter cup to the last galling dregs and said of his work, "It is finished." And so the book of Hebrews says as consequence, "For verily he took not on him the nature of angels," they cannot suffer—"but he took on him the seed of Abraham" (2:16, KJV) that would mean the sweating, suffering inheritance of Adam's children. You remember the old word in Genesis, "In the sweat of thy face shalt thou eat bread." "Wherefore in all things it behoved him to be made like unto his brethren, that he might be a merciful and faithful high priest . . . for in that he himself hath suffered being tempted, he is able to succour them that are tempted" (Hebrews 2:17-18, KJV). His work, his suffering, and his Lordship were all indissolubly joined together. As with our Lord, so it must be with us—there is no other way.

My Brooklyn colleague, Dr. Sandy Ray, has told of his last year at Morehouse College. He said he had absolutely no money and did not see at all how he would graduate. He went to the revered president, Dr. John Hope, and told him his plight. "Go over and see Dr. Archer," said Dr. Hope, referring to the Morehouse officer in charge of student accounts. Well, it worked out. Years later Dr. Archer preached for Dr. Ray and told the people and the preacher about that occasion long ago. He said that Dr. Hope had sent word to him saying, "Press this young man for all he is worth, but don't turn him loose." This is doubtless some of what your days and years are all about. There is One who knows all about us and who cares most deeply for us. There is One who is intent on bringing us to the high and holy destiny which he has in store for us. So, now and again, he presses us for all we are worth and in so doing greatly enlarges our worth. When he has finished his work in us, we shall have, praise God, "come . . . unto a perfect man, unto the measure of the stature of the fulness of Christ" (Ephesians 4:13, KJV).

On Making It to Dinner

Philippians 3:12-14

Walter B. Shurden

I have a good minister friend who, unfortunately, I don't see much anymore. But in those years in which I saw him regularly, I would meet him and ask blandly, "Hi, John, how are you doing?" More often than not, he would counter, "Well, I made it to dinner." His meaning was clear: he had struggled through another day.

Every Christian has an image or a parable or an experience which he fixes on and which serves as a model for his understanding of Christianity. The church has used the cross. I'm glad, because it

Walter B. Shurden, a native Mississippian, is Associate Professor of Religion, holding the Chair of Southern Baptist Studies at Carson-Newman College. He has taught church history at New Orleans Baptist Theological Seminary, Southern Baptist Theological Seminary, and McMaster Divinity School in Hamilton, Ontario, Canada. He is a graduate of Mississippi College and a Th.D. alumnus of New Orleans Baptist Theological Seminary. Before coming to Carson-Newman College, he served as pastor of the First Baptist Church in Ruston, Louisiana. He has written one book, *Not a Silent People: Controversies That Have Shaped Southern Baptists,* and he has written widely for other Southern Baptist publications. In 1974 he received the Distinguished Faculty Award at Carson-Newman College. He is a member and has served as Past President of the Southern Baptist Historical Society.

stands for what God did and what we must do—struggle, spend lonely nights in Gethsemane, and end up rejected in unpopular causes.

My private symbol of Christianity, however, is a grammar school fight on the East Greenwood Elementary School ground in Greenwood, Mississippi, in 1945. A new boy fell victim to the threats of our resident bully and, not knowing better, the scraggly newcomer took him on. Word spread rapidly: "Bobby's supposed to meet the new boy at the water fountain after school today." At East Greenwood the water fountain outside the main school entrance was our colosseum—where the gladiators did their work! The bell rang, we darted for the fountain, made a big circle for the combatants, made our big "bets," and waited for the pugilists. When they entered the ring and the new fellow balled up his fists, I knew he was in trouble because he pressed his thumb over the top of his index finger like a "sissy." Bobby hit him one lick and knocked him down. The little fellow looked up, crying a mad cry. He took the back of his right hand, and beginning on the left side of his mouth, he wiped away blood and dust and spit. And then—I never shall forget it, for it is my symbol of faith—he got to his feet and waded back into ole Bobby.

So much of my Christian life and yours is like that. Being knocked down, hurt on the outside and the inside, disappointed in who we are, stripped of the self-image that puts us on our feet again, we are inclined to lick our wounds, lie still, and opt for an easier way. Unlike the little bloodied boy on the ground, we don't want to struggle to our feet to enter the fray again.

But life is struggle—even the Christian life. Nothing in life that really matters is automatic. You have to struggle to "make" meaning. That is the testimony of all the saints of all the years.

Read again the lives of the really tall souls in Christian history—St. Augustine, St. Bernard, St. Francis, Martin Luther, John Wesley, Walter Rauschenbusch—and you will see that it is so. They searched and scratched for meaning; they agonized and hurt for it; they pled and beat on the gates of heaven for it. And just about the time they thought they had it, they would make Paul's confession: "I count not myself to have apprehended but . . . I press toward the mark . . ." (Philippians 3:13-14, KJV).

My point is that the saints' search for meaning was a struggle. That ought to give all the rest of us some hope. Michael Novak said, "Life, when it is life, is struggle; when struggle is taken away, life goes flat. . . ."[1] Substitution of a single word in that quotation says what I'm trying to say here: "Christianity, when it is Christianity, is struggle; when struggle is taken away, Christianity goes flat."

Christianity is not all grace. It never was; it never will be. However offensive to those of us who cut our theological teeth on the Reformed tradition, with its overbearing emphasis on God's good grace and sovereignty, Christianity has another side to it—human effort, human freedom, human struggle.

So despite the loftiness of the book of Romans, with its emphasis upon what God has done, the Epistle of James, with its emphasis upon what we must do, is still a part of Holy Writings. But James and its "works" theology is a book that many of us have never really liked. And that's quite amazing, since it is one of the easiest books in the New Testament to understand. We would rather play with something "exciting" like the book of Revelation—the hardest book in the Bible to understand! For as long as we can pit one bizarre interpretation of the anti-Christ over against another, as long as we can argue over things which we really do not know about and which really do not matter—as long as we do all that—we don't have to struggle with the days of our lives; we can fantasize about the millennia to come.

But try as we may to avoid the fact, Christian discipleship takes place in the here and now—in the midst of tons of personal guilt, embarrassing personal hypocrisies, and torn relationships. And to complicate matters, almighty God often seems strangely silent when we need him most. The paraphrase of Novak is correct: "Christianity, when it is Christianity, is struggle; when struggle is taken away, Christianity goes flat."

For the Christian, living with one's self is a struggle. Beneath all of our holy doings and holy words and holy grins, there exists a closet full of agonizing contradictions. We can, for example, be tender to those we don't know, cruel to those we do. We can be considerate one moment, cutting the next; spiritual one day, sensual the next.

Before Soviet Russia made her commitments in World War II, Winston Churchill described that country as "a riddle wrapped in a mystery inside an enigma." Most Christians will tell you—late in the night when honesty comes easier—that they feel that way about themselves.

Those of us who name Jesus as Lord ache for some consistency in the stuff of our lives. To be done with the tension between the angelic and the demonic, between Christ and Adam—that's what we want! But we can't have it, not even if we join up with those who peddle perfection. And we can't for the same reason they can't: it's not available.

What is available—to the Christian, at least—is the call to struggle, to keep working at our lives. What is available is the knowledge that God doesn't give up on Peter; so Peter shouldn't give up on himself. Few things are sadder than a Christian, plagued by the burden of personal contradiction, giving up on himself. It is sad because when you give up on yourself, you leave God with nothing to work with.

After twenty years within the church, I'm convinced that the problem in the lives of most Christians is not that we think too highly of ourselves. Just the opposite! We think too little of ourselves. And that thought has driven some right out of the church! The church didn't drive them out. God didn't drive them out. They drove themselves out with feelings of worthlessness with which they refused to struggle.

I've been told for years by every Christian who got the chance to tell me that "since God accepts me, I should accept myself." I'm sure that is a true *statement.* But it has not always been a true *feeling* of mine. The truth is that I believe God does accept me! Yet I still have trouble accepting myself.

So I've decided to come at the problem another way: to be a Christian means to struggle with my feelings of nonworth, to refuse to run the white flag of surrender over my soul every time I fail to live up to it all. To be a Christian is to learn that all the tattered pieces of my life are not automatically at one because of my conversion. To be a Christian is to say out loud that the evangelism which overpromises performs a monumental disservice to the life of discipleship. Why? Because "Christianity, when it is Christianity, is struggle; and when struggle is taken away, Christianity goes flat."

For the Christian, living with others is struggle too. To become a Christian does not automatically put one at peace with everybody else. To the contrary, it puts us at odds with all those people and institutions who are anti-people. Jesus brings a sword as well as peace.

To become a Christian does not even put Christians at peace with each other. Ask the Christians at dissension-ridden Corinth if it is not so. Ask Barnabas and Paul. Ask Peter and Paul. Ask the fundamentalists and the liberals. Ask the social activists and the charismatics. Sometimes Christians expect too much peace too soon. And we often give up too soon because we have to work at human relationships.

Living with others is a struggle even in the closest of human relationships—the home. Marriages are not made in heaven; they are made on earth by two people who work at making marriage work. "People who pray together stay together" only as long as they work at it! If the church sent newly marrieds off with that word, we might celebrate more silver wedding anniversaries.

For the Christian, life with God is struggle, too. For some few, according to their own testimony, the life of prayer and trust and faith comes easily. But not for most. Read again what is still the greatest of all devotional books—the Old Testament Psalms—and you will hear the groans of godly men searching for more of God.

> "My God, my God, why hast thou forsaken me? Why art thou so far from helping me, and from the words of my roaring?" (Psalm 22:1).
>
> "For mine iniquities are gone over mine head: as an heavy burden they are too heavy for me. . . . I am troubled; I am bowed down greatly" (Psalm 38:4, 6).
>
> "I remembered God, and was troubled" (Psalm 77:3).

After you finish with the Psalms, begin working your way through the devotional classics of the Christian church. From Augustine's *Confessions,* to *The Imitation of Christ,* to Thomas Kelly's *A Testament of Devotion,* you hear the voices of those who struggled to get to know Him better. Martin Luther called it *anfechtung,* a word, says Roland Bainton, for which there is no English equivalent. *Anfechtung* "is all the doubt, turmoil, pang, tremor, panic, despair, desolation, and desperation which invade the spirit of man."[2]

Whether one calls it "the words of my roaring" as did the psalmist, or *anfechtung* as did Luther, or simply "struggle," they all mean the same—finding a meaningful relationship with God is not a "natural" for most. It is spiritual labor! But through the struggle— not in spite of it, but *through* it—one finds both God and meaning. Because "Christianity, when it is Christianity, is struggle; and when struggle is taken away, Christianity goes flat."

Now back to making it to dinner, the cross, and the grammar school fight. Each is crucial because each confesses that struggle is at the core of discipleship. If you ever forget that, if I ever forget that, meaning in the Christian life will forever elude us.

Look for
the Rusty Lining

Philippians 4:4-6

William L. Self

Paul wrote a letter to his favorite church, Philippi, from a
Roman jail, knowing that his death was imminent; and yet in the
fourth chapter he wrote: "Rejoice in the Lord alway: and again I say,
Rejoice." (Now that's interesting coming out of a prison!) "Let your
moderation be known unto all men. The Lord is at hand. Be careful
for nothing;" (That is better stated in some of the newer translations,
"Be not anxious for anything" or "Don't worry about anything.")
"but in every thing by prayer and supplication with thanksgiving let

William L. Self, a native of North Carolina, is pastor of the
Wieuca Road Baptist Church in Atlanta, Georgia. A graduate of
Stetson University, he received his B.D. from Southeastern
Baptist Theological Seminary, Wake Forest, North Carolina, and
his S.T.D. from Candler School of Theology, Emory University.
He has served on the Executive Committee of the Georgia
Baptist Convention, as President of the Georgia Baptist Pastor's
Conference, Vice-President of North Carolina Baptist State
Convention, on the Southern Baptist Foreign Mission Board, as
a trustee of Shorter College, and is listed in *Who's Who in
Religion.* He is the author of two books: *Bridging the Generation
Gap,* and with his wife, *Survival Kit for the Stranded.* He has
received honorary degrees from three universities and was
special ambassador for the U.S. government at the inauguration
of President William R. Tolbert of Liberia.

your requests be made known unto God. And the peace of God, which passeth all understanding, shall keep your hearts and minds through Christ Jesus" (Philippians 4:4-7, KJV).

Everyone seems to have a hobby. It may be golf, fishing, hiking, needlepoint. Sometimes a hobby can become one's vocation. There are some people who have a very interesting hobby. They once worried as a hobby but have become so adept that now they are professional worriers. You may think you qualify for that club, but it is highly unlikely that you are in that league yet. You worry about things like orphans, the economy, the depression; you worry about not having a job, your children, your husband (or wife), or your business. All of these things are too ordinary for those who really go at this matter in a very committed way. If you're really going to worry, don't waste your time on things like the government, the economy, airplane crashes, hungry orphans, and that sort of thing. Anybody can worry over these things.

For years we've been told to look for the silver lining. Anybody can do that. If you're determined to worry, you should join the Rusty Lining Society and get your glum genes really working. A report from the Institute of Advanced Sciences at Princeton University stated that there are some stars that are dying and creating black holes in the universe. The professor who did the research speculated that if enough of these stars die, they will suck up the entire universe. How's that for something to worry about every night? Don't worry about hungry children; think about being sucked up into the black holes in the universe!

Now if that doesn't grab you, let me give you another one. If you're going to look for a rusty lining, I want you really to look for a good one. Do you know that the polar ice cap is melting and if it melts at the right time, it could flood the entire Eastern United States? Now that bothers you! You go to bed at night and you wonder: what's the temperature, Lord? You watch the news every night. Is it going to be too hot? Is that polar ice cap going to flood us out of here?

Here is one that seems to bother people more than the polar ice cap or the black holes in the universe. Do you know that the African killer bee in Brazil is migrating north? If you were thinking of running off to South America, look out, because the African killer bee from North Brazil is moving up Central America. You could be stung to death in an Alfred Hitchcock thriller if you go down there!

Most of us have a worry factory in full production inside us.

When we find that production is slow, we think of new things to worry about. It just keeps putting out a product on the assembly line every day. Most of us are members of the kingdom of worry. We have taken out a charter membership, and we carry its passport with us all the time. Jesus knew that. When Jesus was giving that great sermon which we have called the Sermon on the Mount, he looked around and saw all those people carrying burdens. I don't know what they worried about in the first century, but it was probably something just about as important or as significant as the things I have mentioned. Jesus said: Look, don't worry about food, clothing, and shelter. All of these things the Gentiles worry about. You're part of the kingdom of heaven. Your Father is going to take care of you. "Seek ye first the kingdom of God and his righteousness," and he'll take care of these other things for you. Our Lord delivered us from this burden. Our Lord took those rusty linings and polished them up. He said that we don't have any right to spend energy pushing these worries around at night (or whenever it is you do your worrying). Our Lord said for us to quit looking for rusty linings. He said that we are not to be under the tyranny of King Worry.

Paul wrote some words that really strike home. They become more vivid when you realize that he was in a jail when he wrote them. To this little old church at Philippi he said, "Don't be anxious about anything." He put his finger on their anxiety, made a suggestion and a promise. Now the suggestion was this: just quit worrying. Quit being anxious. We have to take the word "anxious" and look at it. The word "anxious" is not just pacing the floor and being upset over something. "Anxious" has the sense of being pulled apart, a feeling that all the things that are coming in on us are just pulling us in a thousand different directions. We're caught between our family, our work, and the traffic. We're caught between our ambition and our frustration. If we don't watch it, we can be anxious over just about anything.

Not long ago I was making a left turn at a busy corner in our neighborhood. I've spent ten years going around that corner and I'll turn it as I please. You get that feeling after awhile. I always watch the light—there's a left-turn signal there—and I had my eye on it. I'm color blind, but I can see an arrow no matter what color it is. It wasn't a split second; it was simultaneous with the turning of that light, when the car behind me let me know that the light had turned. Now I had several alternatives—one was to put it in reverse! The other was to be a fine, safe driver; so at ten miles an hour I turned the corner and went on down the street. You should have seen the expression on the driver's face as he went by! He was anxious about a lot of things when he went by me. In our urban culture we get anxious about everything. I wonder where he was going in such a hurry—probably to hurry up and wait somewhere.

Turn it over to God, Paul says. It's very clear. This is as pedestrian as it can be. When you're dealing with anxiety, whatever it is, the black holes in the sky, the killer African bees in Brazil, or the melting ice cap, you just turn it over to God. Many good Christian people say: "You know I can't pray about that; I'm not going to worry God with my little problem." How would you like it if your children carried a burden and never told you about it? Jesus said that God is our Father; so take what you have and tell him about it. Make your prayer requests known unto God with supplication and thanksgiving. The word "supplication" has as its base the sense of trust. You're opening your heart; you're not hiding anything; you're telling God exactly how you feel. If you're mad at him, tell him. If you don't understand how he runs the universe, tell him. If he's given you what you consider to be a vacuum in life, tell him. Your Father who knows all will begin to move in there next to you and help you carry whatever it is. Paul says: "Let your supplication be known with thanksgiving in everything." He didn't say "the big things"; he didn't say "the medium things"; he said "in everything." If it bothers you, tell your Father about it. Why do we have to be encouraged to pray? We are God's children. The strange thing about it is that we talk a better game about prayer than we ever get around to exercising. God is ready to deal with us if we will just open our lives to him. There have been some who have sown seeds of poor doctrine with us about prayer. They have tried to tell us that prayer is a vending machine: Put in a prayer; get something out immediately. Prayer doesn't work that way. Prayer is a growth experience. God does do explicit things and sometimes God does long-range things, but he *always* gives us the answer to the substance of our prayers. If God answered explicitly every prayer that went to him, the universe would be in chaos. But God has promised us in Jesus that with our praying there will come his positive loving answer. It is interesting to see how God can change people and things when we begin to pray instead of worrying. Supplication is a petition for the supply of our wants. Tell God what you want and need and let him take care of it.

I've decided to let God take care of the swarming African killer bees coming up from Brazil, because I can't do anything about that. I've also decided that God can take care of the hours of the day and the pressures upon our lives.

I remember reading about an old man who lived in a resort community in western North Carolina. Every day he went to the post office to get his mail. Everyone in the community knew that he was way past seventy, but he seemed to have the lift in his life of a man in his fifties. One day a reporter asked him, "Sir, what is the secret of your vitality?" The man looked at him, his eyes flashed, and he said: "The secret of my vitality is understanding New Testament Greek. I used to read the Scriptures and the King James says, 'Take no thought for the morrow.' I couldn't live without thinking about tomorrow; so I began studying the original language. The original language says don't be worried and anxious about tomorrow. I decided I'd quit being anxious about it and let God take care of tomorrow and, strangely enough, the tomorrows sort of got in line. So I don't worry. God has it now. I can go on about other things."

That's the suggestion that Paul makes. Now what is the promise? The promise is one of the most vivid promises of the New Testament. We don't take the promises of God seriously enough. We wait until we're backed in a corner and then expect instant help.

Can you imagine a man in a Roman jail saying: "Make your supplication known to God with thanksgiving and the peace of God which transcends human understanding shall guard your heart"? We make a big deal over the peace of God that goes beyond all understanding, but that's a reality. That's something that all of us want in our lives—a sense of God's peace that transcends the understanding of this world. That is what I want to recommend to you today. There are too many people who have found the tranquil neutrality that comes from tranquilizers and the use or misuse of liquor; there are too many people who have tried to find some kind of tranquillity by the use of one diversion after another, or who have found illicit sexual behavior does not bring peace with anybody.

By running after all of these false prophets of peace, our lives have been crushed. Well, how do you have real peace? True peace is defined best by a story. Two artists were commissioned to paint their conception of what peace really is. Each one went into his studio and worked for the allotted time. The great day came when the paintings were to be viewed. The veiled canvases were placed on easels in the gallery, and the first artist threw the veil off his painting. Everyone present smiled and took a deep breath because the tranquil pastoral scene almost exuded the delightful odors of suppertime, hot biscuits, freshly mowed hay, and the contented lowing of the farm animals being fed in the barn. What could be better than a family working in harmony with nature?

The critics, each lost in his desire to be pulling his chair up to the family table laden with good, plain food, reluctantly turned to view the other canvas depicting peace. They were jolted out of their reveries by the scene of a raging, torrential waterfall cascading, exploding, crashing on the rocks. A gnarled little tree seemed to be clinging to the craggy opening in the rocks. Through the foam and mist you could see a bird's nest precariously perched on the end of a limb stretched out over the falls. There on the nest in the midst of the crashing, thundering torment was a mother bird singing her heart out. This is the peace that transcends human understanding. The peace of God is inward and that is what we are promised. Peace doesn't depend on the traffic, government, or finances; peace depends on the relationship we have with God.

I like the last phrase Paul gives us. He says the peace of God will guard your heart. Paul, you remember, is in jail and there are Roman soldiers all around him. The word used here is "garrison." "And the peace of God will 'garrison' your heart." Every day at the changing of the guard Paul watched them come and go. He was very aware that he was being guarded by those Roman soldiers. Suddenly it occurred to him that God had set soldiers around his heart. He began to think how the peace of God had come and surrounded him, had built a wall around him so that nobody could get in and bother him. Here is a soldier called "hope"; over here is one called "love"; here is one called "patience"; and over here is one called "faith." These garrisoned Paul all the time, keeping out all the anxiety.

When my wife and I were invited to Korea by the prime minister, there were many surprises involved. One surprise was the security guard who was assigned to us. No matter where we went, there he was. Even at night, there was a guard posted outside our door. I didn't like it at first, but then I realized that he was there to protect us—to keep us from being disturbed. Now if a political ruler can set a guard over a guest, just think what God can do for your heart.

The peace of God guards the door of your heart. God set that guard there. It's a garrison of spiritual soldiers to keep the worry genes out. By the grace of God it can be yours if you just open yourself to him with prayer, supplication, and thanksgiving. In the midst of all the turmoil that is going on around you, you can sing your heart out in praise to God.

The Victory God Gives

1 Corinthians 15:35-57

Luther Joe Thompson

> Surgeons must be very careful
> When they take the knife!
> Underneath their fine incisions
> Stirs the Culprit,—Life![1]
> —Emily Dickinson

"The Culprit—Life!" What is so precious or so fragile as "the Culprit—Life"? The poet has said that "our years are as a tale that is told," and indeed, they are, and ironically, by the time we learn to live them, they are finished. Perhaps there is nothing that makes us so

---

Luther Joe Thompson, pastor of the First Baptist Church, Richmond, Virginia, is a native Tennessean, a summa cum laude graduate of Carson-Newman College. He received his Th.M. degree from Southern Baptist Theological Seminary and his Ph.D. degree from the University of Edinburgh, Scotland. He has served on numerous denominational boards and agencies including Midwestern Baptist Theological Seminary, the Golden Gate Baptist Theological Seminary, and the University of Richmond. He has served as visiting preacher at the Ridgecrest and Glorieta Baptist assemblies, as Gheens Lecturer on Preaching at Southern Baptist Theological Seminary, and as guest preacher for the United States Air Force in Spiritual Life Conferences. He has twice received the George Washington Honor Medal for outstanding sermons, and is the author of two books, *Monday Morning Religion* and *Through Discipline to Joy*.

conscious of the preciousness of life as death, and for that very reason people have always been concerned about it.

This concern is expressed in a variety of ways. An older friend confessed the other day, "I am afraid to die"; a twenty-three-year-old, killed in an accident, had his $4,000 motorcycle buried with him; a wealthy spinster left her fortune to her cat. The expressions are as bizarre and unusual as the opinions about life after death. And there is the anguish and searching that tragedy brings: the tragic automobile accident, the businessman who suffers a fatal coronary, the child who dies so abruptly and so illogically. Is the contemporary preoccupation with the weird and bizarre a mere reflection of our neglect of basic biblical truth concerning the life after death?

The biblical revelation confronts the problem of death with disarming candor and positive reassurance. The Old Testament makes very vivid the mystery and enigma of it all. And the New Testament confronts it as the last enemy which must be conquered, but at the same time, as a gateway into a fuller and richer life. There is a Christian perspective concerning life and death, and the believer, even in the twentieth century, needs to understand it. The questions we ask are the same questions men and women were asking in Paul's day, and Paul's answers are still the best we know.

How would you characterize the life after death? Long ago Francis Bacon wrote: "Men fear death as children fear to go in the dark."[2] And later, "It is as natural to die as to be born; and to a little infant, perhaps, the one is as painful as the other."[3] Homer, in *The Iliad,* alludes to sleep and death as twin brothers, and the Orthodox Jew, upon awakening each day, thanks God for restoring him to life again. Seneca, the Roman philosopher, said, "No man enjoys the true taste of life, but he who is ready and willing to quit it."[4]

William Cowper was so right when he wrote:

"Far happier are the dead, methinks, than they
Who look for death, and fear it every day."[5]

Someone has said, "The ancients dreaded death: the Christian can only fear dying." The Christian looks forward to something beyond death. Do you remember Wordsworth's poem?

I have seen
A curious child, who dwelt upon a tract
Of inland ground, applying to his ear
The convolutions of a smooth-lipped shell;
To which, in silence hushed, his very soul

Listened intensely; and his countenance soon
Brightened with joy; for from within were heard
Murmurings whereby the monitor expressed
Mysterious union with its native sea.
Even such a shell the universe itself
Is to the ear of Faith; and there are times,
I doubt not, when to you it doth impart
Authentic tidings of invisible things. [6]

"Authentic tidings of invisible things." There are times when all of us hear them. Jeremy Taylor once wrote: "The more we sink into the infirmities of age, the nearer we are to immortal youth. All people are young in the other world." [7] (No doubt he was thinking of the excitement, the aspiration, the exhilaration, the hope of youth.)

However, it would be foolish indeed to ignore the pain and anguish of bereavement. It is real, it is difficult, it is heartrending. It strikes at the deepest roots of human existence and can release hitherto undiscovered strengths. Like all other fears, the fear of dying and separation needs to be confronted directly with candor and honesty. We need to work through our ambivalent feelings about death and dying. A confronted fear is nearly always easier to bear than one that is pushed to the recesses of the mind.

To learn to accept our mortality is the first step in overcoming it. It is a strange paradox, like finding life by giving it away. The very acceptance of my humanity makes it more precious and helps me to see it in proper perspective. The very fact that my years are temporary adds excitement and exhilaration to the living of them in the present. Indeed, there have been those who have felt that endless years would be intolerable.

In the New Testament writings our mortality is always viewed in the context of the "power of an endless life." We are pilgrims here, and God has infused this present order with the meaning, the purpose, and the power of eternity. Faith gives life on earth a kind of timelessness.

Perhaps it is this very perspective that helps us to get a more biblical understanding of what is entailed in the concept of heaven for the believer. There is the joy of forgiveness; a sense of being clean, accepted, and free; the comfort of belonging to God's family; and the wonder of being loved and loving. There is the knowledge that our work is not in vain and the joy of being with Christ, living in his kind of world, and practicing his kind of life. No doubt Jeremy Taylor's concept, while appealing in his day, was only partial. Surely the life with God entails not only the dreams and health of youth, but also the productivity and satisfactions of maturity and the serenity and peace of age, plus an endless openness to that which is new and growing.

There is great comfort in these matters in the measure of God's grace and the resiliency of the human spirit. All pastors and physicians are keenly aware of the heroism and the strength of the human spirit in the presence of agony and the astonishing ways that God's love seems to reveal itself in such lonely hours.

The questions of 1 Corinthians 15:35 (KJV): "But some will say, How are the dead raised up? and with what body do they come?" are the questions we ask. And Paul's answers are the best we know. It is well to remember that his passage is set right in the center of Paul's great declaration concerning the miracle of the resurrection. The Jews had long debates concerning the future life. The Greeks believed in the immortality of the soul, not the resurrection of the body. "Don't get overly involved with bodily structures," in effect Paul warns. "The only way a seed that you plant can live is for it to die. Death precedes life. A seed is buried and in due process the germ of life is activated and a new plant emerges. It is the same but it is different. It is the same with our bodies. At best the body that is buried is only a bare kernel when compared to the body that is raised. And it is God who gives the body appropriate for the heavenly existence."

Paul sets forth four antitheses to show the difference between the body that dies and the body that is raised from the dead. The body that dies is perishable, or subject to decay, because it is part of the world that is passing away. The body that is raised is imperishable, free from corruption, and able to realize the fullness of life willed by the Creator. The body that is buried is characterized by dishonor or humiliation and wretchedness, while the body that is raised is marked by glory or splendor. The body that dies is stamped by weakness, physical and spiritual, and is the victim of death, while the body that is raised is marked by power or strength given by Him who is able to perform resurrection. The body that dies is a physical body, subject to the limitations of the mortal creature, while the body that is raised is spiritual, animated by the Spirit of God and eternal as God is eternal. A body that is spiritual is one that is made vital by God's Spirit and fitted for the age to come. Our best example is Jesus' resurrected body. He was the same yet different.

It is important to note that for Paul there is no conflict between body and soul. This distinction was entirely a Greek concept. For the Jew, body stands for the whole human being. The great apostle's distinction is not between mortal body and immortal soul, but between the redeemed and the unredeemed. The teachings of this remarkable passage are enough for a lifetime of consideration. The resurrected body will be superior in every way. Human identity will continue. The limitations we know now will be removed. The body will be appropriate for its purpose and, above all, it will be a resurrected body.

Finally, Paul indicates that he has a mystery to convey, a message beyond human comprehension concerning that great eschatological event. There is a great day coming! History moves with purpose and God reigns. Every declaration in the final verses of this remarkable chapter is striking. It is sin that gives death its horror. It makes us cling to our days, want to undo them, face them with anguish. It is God who cleanses and forgives us and gives us the victory through Jesus Christ, our Lord. Apparently Paul does not really mean immortal by nature, but only by the grace of God, and it is God's action that makes possible the final victory. The heart of the matter lies in the victory God gives. It is a victory over fear, defeat, alienation, violence, disease, and death. At this point the early church astonished the world. An ancient writer expressed it: "They bear their dead away with singing as if going to a feast."

There is a grim little verse sometimes intoned by children in their play: "Doctor, Doctor, will I die? Yes, my child, and so will I." That somehow is an improbable notion that a doctor should die. A doctor is alleged to be an expert in matters of life and death and if a doctor cannot offer protection against death, who can? To a security-hungry culture it is disconcerting!

The victory God gives rings true in so many different areas of our human life. We intuitively sense that a person is too valuable to experience only these brief, vulnerable years upon earth. Human relationships are too precious and the very cycle of life itself in the natural world and in us seems to confirm our confidence in tomorrow. One of my most moving experiences in this connection came years ago at the funeral service for an aged Indian father and grandfather. It was an awesome and moving experience. The old man had made his discipleship decision very slowly, but when once it was made, there was no turning back. Before he died, he gathered his family about him like an aged patriarch and said to them, "My children, I am going home. Please remember to be loyal to the Savior." Both his son and his grandson were Christian ministers and participated in the funeral service. The old man's daughter-in-law, formerly a famous Indian beauty, sang "The Indian Love Call," and the son arose and in firm, slow words said: "Our father did three things for us. He gave us the confidence that God could be trusted; he gave us a walk that we could follow with assurance; he gave us the faith that he embodied."

William Cowper, the hymn writer, believed that seventy years were much too brief for full fruition even in human relationship; so he ended a letter to a dear friend: "You must know that I should not love you half so much if I did not know that you would be my friend for all eternity."[8] The first believers were convinced that the love of God for us in Jesus Christ was much too precious for these brief years upon earth and that a whole eternity would be required to experience and express it adequately. That was what they meant by "the power of an endless life."

This is the victory that God gives.

Hope Along with Me

1 Peter 1:1-7

W. Randall Lolley

Someone has said that ours will go down as the generation of the four-letter word. When I first heard that, I did not like the sound of it, but upon further reflection I would not mind being a member of a four-lettered-word generation. For example, "sing" has four letters and so has "care." "Lift" has four letters and so does "pray." "Live" has four letters; so has "love." "Cure" has four letters, and so does "hope." It's that last four-lettered word that I want to highlight here.

Do you remember the barnyard caper which we first heard in

W. Randall Lolley, a native of Troy, Alabama, is President of Southeastern Baptist Theological Seminary in Wake Forest, North Carolina. A graduate of Samford University, he received his B.D. and Th.M. degrees from Southeastern Baptist Theological Seminary and his Th.D. from Southwestern Baptist Theological Seminary. Before assuming the seminary's presidency, he was pastor for twelve years of the First Baptist Church in Winston-Salem, North Carolina. Among his many denominational and community services, he has been President of the North Carolina Baptist Pastor's Conference, a trustee of Campbell College, a member of the Executive Committee of the Southern Baptist Convention, and President of the Conference on Religion, Race, and Community Life in Winston-Salem. He has written articles and curriculum materials and is the author of *Crises in Morality.* In 1971 Wake Forest University conferred upon him the D.D. degree.

childhood? It happened this way. One day Henny Penny was picking up corn in the chicken yard when "whack!" something hit her on the head. "Goodness gracious," she said, "the sky's a'falling; I must go and tell the King." So away she went. Speeding along the route to see the King, she met

> Cocky Locky,
> Ducky Daddles,
> Goosey Poosey,
> Turkey Lurkey.

Each one joined her in the journey to find the King. At long last the expeditioners encountered another who wanted to go along with them. He was Foxy Woxy. Of course, he knew a shortcut on the way to see the King. It led to a narrow and dark hole which turned out to be Foxy Woxy's cave.

The cunning fox advised that one by one the party follow him into the narrow passageway. They cooperated! And in turn each one lost his head forthrightly to end up on Foxy Woxy's dinner table. Henny Penny sensed the situation just in the nick of time. So she turned tail and headed for home. She never reached the King to tell him the sky was falling. The fact is, when she returned to the barnyard, she discovered that it had been an acorn which hit her on the head.

Here is a tale that speaks of the times. There always seems to be some Henny Penny telling a Cocky Locky, Ducky Daddles, Goosey Poosey, Turkey Lurkey, as well as anyone else who will listen, that the sky is falling. The practical effect of this dismal report is that people everywhere are losing hope, and they are being led by all kinds of cunning Foxy Woxys into all kinds of dark, narrow holes in the ground.

The situation has developed even among Christians. In the church, as elsewhere, hope has become a casualty. For a half century all sorts of theological Henny Pennys have had only one word for either the king or the commoner—"the sky's a'falling." Consequently the whole field of Christian thought became a quagmire of despair. Until the German theologian Jürgen Moltmann came along recently, we had no "theology of hope." The slough of despond had claimed us.

Have you sensed just how thorough and permeating hopelessness has become nowadays? Hope, like some gigantic Humpty Dumpty, has indeed fallen off the wall, and it seems that all the king's horses and all the king's men can't put it back together again.

Cynicism is in. Hope is out. That is to say that the tide is running against the hoper and for the raw realist.

Even well-intentioned Christians have all but banished hope from far more than just their vocabularies. They haven't meant to do this, but it has happened nevertheless. I wonder how it has happened and why. Perhaps a brief historical review will suffice to give us clues regarding reasons. Remember? This twentieth century dawned in a splash of empty and immoral optimism, but it has been dashed upon hard anvils during this first three-quarters of the century.

For example, the century cascaded in with everybody ready to get on an escalator going up, up, and away toward Utopia. The counsel was that all we needed on the planet Earth was a little more time, a little more money, and a little more energy, and we would build ourselves "a never-never land" right here on the earth and would live happily ever after.

Then, not even twenty years into the century, Johnny went marching off to World War I to fight the war that would end all wars. When he returned home, he and his generation soon bogged down in the throes of economic depression which in time became an international phenomenon. You know what brought us out of that depression? Ultimately it was World War II which did it. Johnny went marching off again midway into the century to fight another war that would end all wars. Upon his return home this time, he found inflation doing about the same thing to his dollars that the depression had done previously. To make bad matters worse, then came Korea and after that we were bogged down in the jungles of Southeast Asia until now the topsy-turvy economy features a depressed inflation or an inflated depression. In any case, it's a phenomenon we've never encountered before.

The practical result of all this is that the illusion of automatic and inevitable progress has been seen for what it is—sheer paganism. It has been exposed as trust in a pantheon of false gods who "hast set their glory amongst steel mills and cyclotrons." Multitudes have sensed that this muddled optimism never was reliable, much less Christian. So, there has been an honest effort to compensate—even to overcompensate.

In reaction against the empty and immoral optimism of the early part of this century, it has been established now that any kind of hoping just has to be regarded as juvenile idealism and illusion. It may be all right for timid and retarded souls to hope but not for full grown he-men and she-women facing reality. The times thus belong to the Henny Pennys in search of someone to tell that the sky is a'falling. Very few look any longer for an "impossible possibility," and I want to raise a protest against such despair.

Not too long ago, in Charles Schulz's remarkable *Peanuts* comments on life, Charlie Brown encountered loud-mouthed Lucy sitting in her psychiatric booth where all kinds of advice can be acquired yet for a nickel. She said as he approached, "Charlie Brown, I've been thinking about your situation." He responded, "Well, I'm grateful to learn that." To which she replied, "I've decided that what you need is a philosophy of life—something that will see you through times of stress. I want you to think and think and think until you come up with one." Then for a couple of frames Charlie Brown, that twentieth-century everyman with a T-shirt of thorns, did think. Finally he concluded, "I've got it, life is like an ice-cream cone; you've got to learn to lick it." To that, Lucy responded, "Well, that's the most stupid philosophy of life I've ever heard." Charlie Brown walked dejectedly away from the booth muttering, "It's hard to come up with a good philosophy of life in less than twenty seconds."

Charlie Brown is right! Therefore let's not tempt ourselves with a philosophy of life developed with a lick and a promise and a rushed up prayer, but rather let's share a proclamation. We must remember that the living God has a million miracles he hasn't used up yet, and he wants us to be some of them.

Have you noticed how that lilting word "hope" skips and sings all the way through the New Testament? You can no more miss it than you can miss the Atlantic Ocean while sailing in a craft on its waves.

Paul picks up this recurring refrain with his blessing in Romans: "The God of hope fill you with all joy and peace in believing" (15:13, KJV). Banish that conviction from Scripture and you have severed the jugular vein of original Christian faith. The person is right who said that early Christians did not cringe in corners and mutter, "Look what our world has come to," but rather they looked into the teeth of danger and exclaimed, "Look what has come to the world."[1]

Hope is the soul's invincible surmise: faith and hope and love sink or swim together in every believer. Lose the capacity to hope, and it is not long until both faith and love suffer. As long as one hopes realistically, one can live abundantly. But that is precisely our problem. The ring of the real is missing from so many of our hopes. We are like old Sinbad the sailor who anchored his craft to what he thought was a sturdy atoll, only to discover that it was a big fish which dashed off with sailor, craft, and all. That is precisely our situation. We have anchored our hopes to false supports so long that we would scarcely know the real thing if we encountered it.

It is time to meet once more the real thing; so let's go to the head of the class to do it. Allow the writer of Peter to introduce us to what he calls "a living hope. . . ." Never forget the times were tough as nails when these words were originally written. There was sand in all the soup. Rome ruled all the real estate and had her heels on the necks of the citizens. Yet in one corner of Asia the little church of Jesus Christ had started to grow. Rome decided that this upstart bunch of hotheads and hot-hearts who were outliving and outdying the opposition had best be stamped out. So Christians were labeled outlaws. They lost their jobs, their freedoms, and thousands of them were brutally slain. Those who followed Christ were laying their lives on the line. It's no accident then that some of them were losing hope. They were justifiably frightened at what the future held for them. It was to these kinds of persons in those kinds of times that the writer originally wrote this epistle of hope.

It is a strong and urgent word to all who are about to lose heart. What did he say to them and thus to us? There are at least two things that are especially urgent just now:

First, the author reminds us that in moments of extreme difficulty Christians have their best opportunity to live for Christ in this world. You see, tough times are not times for the people of God to want out of life, but to want into it deeper. Christians have always had more formulas for dealing with adversity than they have had for dealing with prosperity.

Therefore, instead of shouting for the world to stop so we can get off, this author reminds us to look for places to get on. Hear the strong word of the Lord: "Praise be to the God and Father of our Lord Jesus Christ, who in his great mercy gave us new birth into a living hope by the resurrection of Jesus Christ from the dead!" (1 Peter 1:3, NEB).

"A living hope . . ."—that says it. But note this: the hope lives when it is fastened on to the fact of a Christ who has conquered death. Christians in this world live for that conquering Christ, not for themselves. They hope in him, not in themselves. Hope comes trickling, running, and finally surging back into a life as one serves Christ in the world where one is.

Our problem is like theirs in ancient Asia. When tensions tighten, we are ready to throw in the sponge, call the game, turn out the lights, and go home. That's when we need to listen to this time-tested counsel. Hope happens when persons put their hands to the tasks that must be done in Christ's name in their times. Hopelessness is the result of two factors converging at once in the experience of a believer. The first is a fading vision of God, and the second is a failing duty in human relationships. When the people of God quit their unique work in the world, they lose hope. But so long as the people of God keep at the work which is theirs in their times, hope is a real live possibility.

The second thing that the author says is this: in moments of most extreme difficulty the people of God stand to learn from tough times.

Listen to the time-tested counsel: "This is cause for great joy, even though now you smart for a little while, if need be, under trials of many kinds. Even gold passes through the assayer's fire, and more precious than perishable gold is faith which has stood the test. These trials come so that your faith may prove itself worthy of all praise, glory, and honour when Jesus Christ is revealed" (1 Peter 1:6-7, NEB). We are to learn the lessons taught by tough times. Deep in the heart of this universe there is a cross-principle. Jesus spoke of it in his metaphors of seed, salt, leaven, and light. It is the principle by which life comes through dying.

That principle speaks to hopelessness. It has a word for a broken heart. You see, this is a visited planet. Suffering can be redemptive. Jesus Christ at Golgotha proved that. Tough times do indeed have universal lessons to teach.

One of the chief lessons to be learned from difficulty is that God used broken things in all his miracles. For example, broken clouds produce rain; broken soil produces crops; broken seed produces grain; broken grain produces bread; broken bread produces strength. This indicates that God can use a broken life, but he must have all the pieces.

Historian Charles A. Beard was asked what major lessons his study of history had taught him. This was his reply: "First, whom the gods would destroy, they must first make mad with power. Second, the mills of God grind slowly; yet they grind exceedingly small. Third, the bee fertilizes the flower it robs. And fourth, when it's dark enough, you can see the stars."[2]

We can listen to the hardheaded historian. His is a lesson taught by the ages. Suffering and stars do somehow go together. There are yet some things in this tired, jaded world worth looking for, suffering for, and even hoping for.

The *Man of La Mancha* is a contemporary musical update of the old Don Quixote story. Dulcinea is a sad little woman of the streets. At one point in that fine musical she asks Don Quixote why he's always caring when no one else seems to, why he's always involved when it isn't really his fight, and why he always keeps giving when it seems so right to take. The Man from La Mancha answers her inquiry with some words which tell of his impossible dream to keep on keeping on in his glorious quest to reach the difficult and unreachable goals of life.

You see, God does not expect us just to believe in miracles; he expects us to be one. So let's be a miracle person in the toughest of times. Come, hope along with me—in the living Christ!

A Ticket to Wherever It Is

Ecclesiastes 1:14; Matthew 16:24-26

William P. Tuck

The place—a commuter train. The time—midnight. Loren Eiseley, an anthropologist, recounts the episode. He boarded a train in New York and felt glad to be leaving the city. On taking a seat in the smoking compartment, his eyes fell on a gaunt, shabbily dressed man, who was sitting with his eyes closed and his head thrown back on the seat. A paper sack was on the man's lap. The man appeared to be drowsing either from exhaustion or from liquor. As the train wound its way out of the city, the conductor came into the compartment

William P. Tuck, a native of Virginia, is presently pastor of the First Baptist Church in Bristol, Virginia, and Adjunct Professor of Religion and Philosophy at Virginia Intermont College. He is a graduate of the University of Richmond; Southeastern Baptist Theological Seminary, Wake Forest, North Carolina, B.D., Th.M.; and the New Orleans Baptist Theological Seminary, Th.D. He has done additional graduate study at Emory University. Previous pastorates have been in Louisiana and Virginia. He has been active in denominational and civic affairs and served as a trustee of Virginia Intermont College. In 1974, he was awarded the Man and Boy Award from the Bristol Boys' Club. He is the author of *Facing Grief and Death,* which was published in 1975, and has had articles published in magazines, such as *Theology Today, The New Pulpit Digest, The Review and Expositor,* and other denominational publications.

asking for tickets, and everyone turned to watch the derelict. Opening his eyes slowly and fumbling in his pocket until he pulled out a roll of bills, he said, in a deathlike croak, "Give me . . . give me a ticket to wherever it is."

The conductor stood stupefied for a moment with the roll of bills in his hand. He mumbled through the list of stations, but once again the man's eyes were closed, and he remained mute. After a moment the price of a ticket to Philadelphia was deducted from the roll of bills, and they were shoved back into the snoozing man's hand. The train sped into the night as the observers of this incident turned back to their newspapers. "In a single poignant expression," Eiseley notes, "this shabby creature on a midnight express train had personalized the terror of an open-ended universe."[1]

"Give me a ticket to wherever it is." Eiseley has captured in his story a familiar symbol of our situation. We are caught in the current of today's stream of life and simply flow with it, often without any sense of direction or meaning. Like the microscopic plants in the ocean called "plankton," many today are drifting and wandering. "I think I'll go back to Germany," a young student said to me. He had studied there for three years, and, after only six months in this country, he had decided to go back. "I have felt for so long like an outsider looking in. There are many roads a person can travel on. I'll find mine one day." He, too, is traveling to "wherever it is."

The road to "wherever it is" is varied. For some the journey trails off into frustration and pessimism. "What's the point of trying?" the teenager exclaimed. "My parents and teachers never give me a chance; I can't win." "All politicians are crooks," a man observed. "Watergate proves that!" The social worker found a family of eleven living in what used to be a chicken house. "We ain't got nothing," the mother said. "We had to live some place." "You can't escape this ghetto," a youth exclaimed. "We are all trapped here like it was a graveyard."

"Blow-in' in the wind" today are many pessimistic complaints about our country, our cities, world affairs, the economy, the government, the environment, the church, the colleges, young people, old people, and hundreds of other matters. Many feel like the newborn chick, depicted in the cartoon, that pecks its way out of its eggshell, sticks its head out and looks around, and then pulls the broken piece of shell back into place and retreats into the safety of the eggshell. But where is that womb of absolute security, free of difficulties and where every need and wish are satisfied? "Time has expired for them," some say, and they are weary with trying. "Wherever it is" for them is an endless treadmill filled with contradictions, ambiguities, disappointments, and discord.

"Wherever it is" for some ends in despair. Whispers and screams, reminiscent of the Ecclesiastes' preacher, resound from many quarters today. "I have seen everything that is done under the sun; and behold, all is vanity and a striving after wind" (Ecclesiastes 1:14, RSV). Faces, voices, and struggles rush back into my mind, demanding to be heard again and again with a hidden plea for direction out of their darkness. I hear a voice: "What difference would it make if I were not alive?" a young woman asked. "I'm worthless and nobody would miss me." "He walked off and left me and the children for some woman and never looked back," another woman cried. "What do I do now?" An article I read burns in my memory. The elderly couple sat on the sofa in their living room in a rowhouse in South Philadelphia. They had just been robbed. As they told their story, the cracked and stained wallpaper in the room was illuminated by a single, bare, light bulb in a gooseneck lamp. What's so unusual about their story? Are they not just another poor couple getting "ripped off" in a low-income neighborhood? Yes—but more and worse. They are both blind and 104 years old! A child's voice rises out of the rubble of an undeclared war to pierce an unfeeling world. "I'm nobody's nothing," exclaimed the little boy as he glanced up from where he was sitting on top of a pile of debris in war-torn Saigon. His relatives were all dead. He was alone and unwanted in a city already overflowing with homeless children. A young man shouted a challenge that went unanswered. "If anyone can convince me that life is worth living," he cried, as he stood on the narrow ledge seventeen stories above Fifth Avenue in New York City, "I won't jump." He jumped.

The images, unfortunately, could be multiplied endlessly. The number of suicides has greatly increased. Today about twenty thousand people commit suicide each year in the United States alone. Around the world that figure swells to 250,000 men and women. Why? "Behold; all is vanity and a striving after wind," the ancient preacher says. Many seem to find themselves trapped in a dead-end street and see no way to turn. Their yearnings are unfulfilled, their hopes shattered, their dreams punctured, their bodies fatigued, their minds disturbed, their hands empty, their eyes and hearts vacant. The words of a recently disturbing popular song, voiced by a woman singer, ask cynically, after describing several pleasant scenes: "Is that all there is?" It is again the cry of meaninglessness. It is purchasing a ticket to "wherever it is."

Disturbing images march across our line of vision daily. Suicide, war, suffering, unemployment, poverty, hunger, drug addiction, alcoholism, pain, and death stare at us from our TV sets, newspapers, magazines, across the street, next door, the hospital bed, the nursing home, the empty kitchen cabinet, the want ads, our front room, or back bedroom. Questions concerning the meaning of life cannot be hidden or ignored. They are here, and they are real. They frighten and haunt us. They bother and confuse us. And sometimes they challenge us. Are we simply caught in the stream of life and being carried by it? Without a sense of direction we have no hope. In the movie *Bonnie and Clyde,* Bonnie has been enamored by the life of bank robbing and seems to be enjoying it, until one day she reveals a sense of futility about their style of life when she observes: "I thought we were going somewhere, but we are just going."

Our going should have some purpose. People are going, nevertheless. Stand on any busy downtown corner or on a subway platform in New York, Chicago, London, Stockholm, Copenhagen, Hong Kong, or even small town U.S.A., and you will observe that people are going. As you observe these people going on any busy square or round, have you ever wondered, along with me, where are they all going, and what are they doing? What are their dreams and problems, joys and sorrows? I have often watched and reflected as they passed on the street, on the train, or on the plane. I wonder if they are curious about me, as well. Are they probing for a direction, too, or are they just going? Do we continue to look at each other day after day, week after week, and do not know or care about each other? Yes, we are busy going, but is our going filled with direction?

Directions, however, are not always easily given or received, understood or followed. Several years ago on Christmas Eve I had struggled for about an hour trying to put together a riding toy for our small son. Noticing the unhappy results and the several nuts and bolts left over, my wife came over, searched through the cardboard box, came up with a yellow sheet of paper, handed it to me, and smilingly teased, "When all else fails, read the directions." "When all else fails. . . ." Why do we wait until we reach that point? I do not know, but often we do, in large matters as well as small.

If the ticket to nowhere is dispensed with the stamp "All is vanity and a striving after wind," then the ticket to somewhere is imprinted with the penetrating words of Jesus, "If any man would come after me, let him deny himself and take up his cross and follow me. For whoever would save his life will lose it, and whoever loses his life for my sake will find it. For what will it profit a man, if he gains the whole world and forfeits his life? Or what shall a man give in return for his life?" (Matthew 16:24-26, RSV). In the words of Jesus, direction is given. They are, however, words which indicate clearly that the "ticket" which he issues us is not good if detached. Many today suffer a sense of meaninglessness, because they have lost all awareness of absolute transcendence. They refuse to acknowledge any power beyond themselves and defy the believer to prove that God exists. The ancient religious poet was no stranger to this puzzle. "My adversaries taunt me, while they say to me continually, 'Where is your God?'" (Psalm 42:10, RSV). In her childish way, a young girl, as noted in *Children's Letters to God,* expressed the attitude of many cynics when she asked:

"Dear God,

Are you real? Some people don't believe it. If you are, you better do something quick."[2]

The price that anyone pays for the eclipse of God, however, is to be thrown back on one's own resources. This is an aloneness that none can stand. No wonder it leads to despair and cynicism. Do we decide to "write off" God because there are problems and injustices which defy easy answers?

"Look at the mess the world is in," some observe. "What word do we hear from God about it?" What word would they accept? God has already spoken in his incarnate Word, and, if they will not respond to that word, what word will they hear? Those who have "ears to hear" have heard God's coming in that living Word and have responded to it. Life requires of us a decision of commitment. We commit ourselves either to the way of despair and cynicism or to the path of faith and hope. Either choice requires commitment. We select faith or non-faith. We choose to believe or to sneer. We turn to hope or despair. We choose, nevertheless. Even our non-choosing is deciding. Struggle and responsibility are simply a part of the fiber of life. It is still, after all has been said on either side, a leap of trust or non-trust. We can leap into the "slough of despondency" or make a "leap of faith." If we make the leap of faith, we will take up our cross and follow Christ. We have, then, become people of "the way." We also travel this path with an awareness, in the words of Dag Hammarskjöld, that "the way chose you—And you must be thankful."[3]

Last summer my family and I visited King's Dominion, a large amusement park near Richmond, Virginia. Among the many attractions and rides, we decided to take the venture down the giant sliding board. With our sliding sacks in our hands, my wife, seven-year-old son, nine-year-old daughter, and I made the long climb up the steep steps to the top. None of us, however, had anticipated that it would be so high! Catherine, my daughter, took her plunge cautiously; Emily, my wife, lunged forward with some reluctance; Bill Powell sat undecidedly until one of the attendants gave him a helpful shove; I caught my breath, leaned forward, and said to myself, "Here we go, I hope." Some others made the climb to the top, saw how high it was, and quickly retreated down the steps, unwilling to risk the slide. They missed the fun and adventure because they would not take the seemingly risky venture. I wonder how many do not find the thrill of the adventure of life because they have remained trapped in their own corner of self-sufficiency and have not been willing to make the leap of trust? "What is the end of man?" Calvin asked at the beginning of his Catechism. "To know God and love him forever." What is his happiness? The same. We have been created to have fellowship with God, and genuine happiness cannot be realized apart from God. "In him," as Augustine wrote, "we live and move and have our very being." The writer of the Gospel of John noted that the purpose of his gospel was "that you may believe that Jesus is the Christ, the Son of God, and that believing you may have life in his name" (John 20:31, RSV). Jesus tells us that life in him has direction. It is life filled with meaning and purpose. "I am come," Jesus said, "that they might have life, and that they might have it more abundantly" (John 10:10, KJV).

Faith provides us with direction. With our lives rooted and grounded in God, we have a sense of inner strength and stability. We are conscious that the universe is not moving madly along without direction but is under the control of a Creator who is a loving friend, whom we can know and love. William James, the famous professor of philosophy at Harvard, wrote to a friend in January, 1868: "All last winter . . . I was on the continual verge of suicide. . . ."[4] What was it that brought James out of his mental distress? He noted later that when he had been driven to the edge of the slope, with pessimism at the bottom, and the nightmare of suicide as one of the few options left to him, the final appeal to which he turned was his religious faith. As Christians we confront our world, not with naive notions about its conditions, but with an inner joy and faith that does not give way to despair. We enter into life with our eyes wide open to the struggles that people experience, and our ears are filled to the bursting point with the noise of the world, but we still affirm: "Hallelujah! The Lord God Omnipotent reigneth!" With the apostle Paul we declare: "Yet we who have this spiritual treasure are like common clay pots, to show that the supreme power belongs to God, not to us. We are often troubled, but not crushed; sometimes in doubt, but never in despair; there are many enemies, but we are never without a friend; and though badly hurt at times, we are not destroyed" (2 Corinthians 4:7-9, TEV).

Life in Jesus Christ gives us perspective. We often desire to live in an imaginary world, free of struggle and problems, glowing with spectacular events. We sometimes feel that we have been slighted and that someone else has received a better slice of life than we have. We become bogged down in the sameness and routineness of our days and long for something more exciting or dramatic. When suffering or difficulties come our way, we want to cry, "Why me? What have I done to deserve this?" Several summers ago when my daughter fell out of a tree and broke her arm, she looked up from the ground and exclaimed, "I wish this was a bad dream." In times of pain and unpleasantness, we long for escape and relief.

Perspective lifts our horizon. It keeps us from being crushed by circumstances or events. If our vision is determined by outward circumstances, then we might easily be defeated by despair. Our vision is lifted beyond the local and immediate conditions when we are aware that we are committed to a God who allows all free will, but who is slowly, decade by decade and century by century, working out his will in the world. We live with the awareness that God does not exempt the Christian from all suffering and difficulties, but he assures us of his presence in the midst of our struggles. Tribulation, distress, persecution, famine, nakedness, peril, or sword shall not separate us from the love of God. Paul says in his Roman epistle, "No, in all these things we are more than conquerors through him who loved us. For I am sure that neither death, nor life, nor angels, nor principalities, nor things present, nor things to come, nor powers, nor height, nor depth, nor anything else in all creation, will be able to separate us from the love of God in Christ Jesus our Lord" (Romans 8:37-39, RSV).

This kind of inner assurance enabled Dietrich Bonhoeffer, the German theologian, to walk with courage as the Nazi Gestapo led him to the scaffold. "This is the end," he said to his friends before he left, "For me the beginning of life."[5] If we seek to get meaning from life only from the comforts and securities of material things, we will be disappointed. The English word for happiness is derived from a root word which means chance. Happiness, according to this approach, will depend on circumstances, the sands of fortune, or just plain luck. If happiness is primarily an external matter, many circumstances can cause it to disappear, such as the death of a loved one, a financial setback, war, natural calamities, accidents, suffering, or disappointments. The Christian's happiness is founded on internal security which is independent of external circumstances. If our life and happiness are based only on material things, when they are removed, as circumstances often do remove them, then all meaning for living disappears with them. The Christian's security, however, is rooted in the awareness of God's love and providence. It is the "joy" which Jesus said no one can take from you (see John 16:22).

When I lived in New Orleans, I had the opportunity of hearing Viktor Frankl, the Austrian psychiatrist who had spent some harrowing years in Auschwitz and other grim, German concentration camps. He spoke of his search for "a will to meaning" in the midst of these horrid conditions of suffering and inhumanity. Out of his agonizing experience he concluded that a person who has a "why" for living can endure almost any "how." One can survive the worst conditions when one's life has purpose. Frankl is convinced that a person finds meaning in life only "to the extent to which he commits himself to something beyond himself, to a cause greater than himself."[6] In a sense, then, is it not true that a person who commits suicide is one who has become so self-conscious that one cannot see life in any terms beyond one's own existence? Despair arises because everything is measured by our own needs and not by what we can do for others. The "why" is gone, and we are crushed. As Christians we find the "why" to life's meaning beyond our selfish interests when we "lose our lives" in the service of others. As we spend ourselves in service for others, we not only minister to others but also to ourselves.

Many of the words of Jesus are not easy to understand or apply. The words of Jesus often shatter our pretenses for nominal living and challenge us to a higher way. For many, life's motto for happiness is "safety first," and the old maxim, "self-preservation is nature's first law," becomes the standard for defensive living. Jesus has challenged these assertions and has pointed us in a different direction to affirmative living. He guides us to realize that we find life paradoxically by losing it. "For whoever would save his life will lose it; and whoever loses his life for my sake, he will save it" (Luke 9:24, RSV). The reality of life's meaning, according to Jesus, is found in the dedication to something outside of myself with such intense commitment that I forget about myself. Can this be possible? This is the direction to which Jesus points us.

In our century, Albert Schweitzer has exemplified sacrificial dedication. Although he was acclaimed as a noted philosopher, theologian, organist, musicologist, minister, and professor; he believed something was missing from his life. The void in his life was filled when he prepared himself to go as a medical missionary to Lambarené, Africa. Schweitzer believed that he needed to make some acknowledgment to God for the blessings he had received. In his autobiography, he states that he was stabbed awake one morning with the realization that "I must not accept this happiness as a matter of course, but must give something in return for it. . . . I tried to settle what meaning lay hidden for me in the saying of Jesus: 'Whosoever would save his life shall lose it, and whosoever shall lose his life for my sake and the Gospels shall save it.' . . . In addition to the outward, I now had inward happiness."[7] When our lives are directed inwardly, our concerns are selfish, and we cannot see beyond our own immediate needs or desires. So, we rush from one arena of life to another seeking satisfaction and fulfillment. We long to be fed, groomed, entertained, and protected. We are like the Lock in one of Lewis Carroll's fantasies which ran continually and feverishly looking for something. "Why, whatever is the matter?" someone asked the Lock. "I'm looking," replied the Lock, "for a key to unlock me!"[8] The Lock symbolizes every man. It mirrors our own dilemma. Everyone of us longs for someone to come along with the key which will unlock our genuine self and enable us to experience the real meaning of life. Jesus offers us the key to the authentic life in sacrificial living. His paradox provides the key which can unlock our lives. As we follow him, we discover that we save only as we spend ourselves in some cause beyond ourselves; we receive only in giving, and find only by losing.

"The Schweitzers in our world are rare," someone says. Yes, but Albert Schweitzer does not stand alone. Others, from the age of the apostle Paul to our present era, have marched that sacrificial way. Remember Francis of Assisi, the man of peace and poverty; Florence Nightingale, the founder of the modern nursing movement; William Booth, whose Salvation Army circles the world; Martin Luther, the church reformer; Toyohiko Kagawa, the Japanese social reformer; Tom Dooley, the medical doctor to Southeast Asia; Ann Sullivan Macy, who lifted Helen Keller out of a pit of personal darkness; Martin Luther King, Jr., who dreamed of a new, free society for all people. The list could go on. They lost themselves in worthy causes beyond themselves. They found the higher way and dared to walk in it.

I have seen others who have walked the paradoxical way of Jesus. They have received little recognition, if any, for their service— no national or world applause. They saw a need and moved in to help, in a quiet, unheralded manner. You know their faces in your community. In my community, I can see a retired school principal, in her eighties, walking to church in the snow to teach a middle-aged black man how to read, as she has taught hundreds before him. I see a man, whose work schedule is demanding, yet who gives many hours each week to the Boys' Club. I see a couple who bring international students into their home and give them a place where they are loved. I see another couple, going week after week to nursing homes and talking, listening, and playing with the patients. Many others could join this list. They have committed their lives in a quiet manner to the Christlike way. These are the kind of people who have found the direction of God in ordinary living. These are people who "have bloomed where they were planted" and have not spent this time fantasizing about what they could do if—. They have concluded that the problems of life demand daily attention and are not overcome usually in spectacular ways but by plain hard work. They are aware that they cannot solve all the problems of the world or even in their own community, but they have committed themselves to attacking a problem, a part of a problem, if you like, where they live. They are aware that they may not lift the whole burden of sin and suffering from the back of humanity, but they will get under the load so that others will feel some benefit from their efforts. They work with the knowledge that one does not find a meaningful life but makes life meaningful. They are aware that they are few, but they labor with the knowledge that throughout history it has always been a few who have engaged in the struggle against the meaningless forces in the world.

They work with the awareness that they do not labor alone but along with God. Christians link their lives with a cause and a purpose bigger than themselves, "the kingdom of God." They remember the words of their Lord: "Be concerned above everything else with his kingdom and with what he requires, and he will provide you with all these other things" (Matthew 6:33, TEV). No one has all the answers to the questions of suffering, sin, or evil; but, as we move in the light we already have in the way of Jesus Christ, we find more light, and we can then venture into it. In his light we find direction, and we can walk with the assurance that his way is going somewhere.

Notes

PREFACE

[1] Elton Trueblood, *The Life We Prize* (New York: Harper & Row, Publishers, 1951), p. 49.

[2] Albert Camus, *The Myth of Sisyphus and Other Essays,* trans. Justin O'Brien (New York: Alfred A. Knopf, Inc., 1955), p. 3.

[3] Paul Tillich, *The New Being* (New York: Charles Scribner's Sons, 1955), p. 22.

[4] William James, *Essays on Faith and Morals,* selected by Ralph B. Perry (New York: Meridian Books, 1962), p. 8.

A STRATEGY FOR SURVIVAL, *John Killinger*

[1] Theodore Dreiser, *The Financier* in *Trilogy of Desire* (New York: The World Publishing Company, 1972), pp. 3-5.

[2] Piers Paul Read, *Alive: The Story of the Andes Survivors* (New York: J. B. Lippincott Company, 1974), p. 309. © 1974 by Piers Paul Read. Reprinted by permission of J. B. Lippincott Company.

[3] *Ibid.,* p. 84.

[4] *Ibid.,* p. 338.

THE TRUE BELIEVER, *Carlyle Marney*

[1] MacNeile Dixon, *The Human Situation:* Gifford Lectures, 1935–1937 (New York: Longmans, Green and Co.), p. 14.

[2] William James, *Essays on Faith and Morals,* selected by Ralph B. Perry (New York: Meridian Books, 1962), pp. 60-61.

THE FOOLISH THINGS JESUS DID, *Wesley Shrader*

[1] Sigmund Freud, *Civilization and Its Discontents,* trans. and ed. James Strachey (New York: W. W. Norton & Company, Inc., 1961), p. 56. © 1961 by James Strachey.

[2] Quoted in *Ibid.,* p. 57.

THE CROSS IN THE MARKETPLACE, *Foy Valentine*

[1] Virginia Brasier, "Time of the Mad Atom," *Saturday Evening Post,* May 28, 1949, p. 72.

[2] Arthur Miller, *Death of a Salesman* (New York: The Viking Press, Inc., 1949), p. 138.

[3] George F. MacLeod, *Only One Way Left* (Glasgow: The Iona Community, 1956), p. 38.

ON OVERCOMING MORAL FATIGUE, *Samuel D. Proctor*

[1] J. W. Cunliffe et al., *Century Readings in English Literature* (New York: Appleton-Century-Crofts, 1929), p. 862.

A WHOLE MAN MADE WELL, *Frank Stagg*

[1] G. B. Caird, *The Revelation of St. John the Divine,* Harper's New Testament Commentaries (New York: Harper & Row, Publishers, 1966), p. 297.

[2] Herbert Danby, *The Mishnah,* translated from the Hebrew with introduction and brief explanatory notes (London: Oxford University Press, 1933), pp. 100-136.

[3] See Theodor H. Gaster, *The Dead Sea Scriptures, in English Translation* (New York: Doubleday & Company, Inc., 1956), pp. 77-79.

[4] See Abraham J. Heschel, *Who Is Man?* (Stanford, Calif.: Stanford University Press, 1965), p. 29.

[5] For this and other biblical perspectives on human existence, see Frank Stagg, *Polarities of Man's Existence in Biblical Perspective* (Philadelphia: The Westminster Press, 1973).

TO LIVE IS TO LOVE, *Paul D. Simmons*

[1] Viktor Frankl, *Man's Search for Meaning,* rev. ed. (New York: Simon & Schuster, Inc., 1969), pp. 58-59.

[2] Paul Scherer, *Love Is a Spendthrift* (New York: Harper & Row Publishers, 1961).

[3] Thomas Kepler, "Still the Greatest Thing in the World," in *Best Sermons: 1959-1960,* ed. G. Paul Butler (New York: Thomas Y. Crowell Company, 1959), p. 169.

ON MAKING IT TO DINNER, *Walter B. Shurden*

[1] Michael Novak, *Ascent of the Mountain, Flight of the Dove* (New York: Harper & Row, Publishers, 1971), p. 53.

[2] Roland Bainton, *Here I Stand: A Life of Martin Luther* (Nashville: Abingdon Press, 1950), p. 42.

THE VICTORY GOD GIVES, *Luther Joe Thompson*

[1] Martha Dickinson Bianchi and Alfred Leete Hampson, eds., *Poems by Emily Dickinson* (Boston: Little, Brown and Company, 1942), p. 22.

[2] Francis Bacon, *Essays: Of Death,* cited by Howell and Ray in *The Macmillan Book of Proverbs, Maxims, and Famous Phrases,* selected by Burton Stevenson (New York: Macmillan Publishing Co., Inc., 1965), p. 515.

[3] Francis Bacon, *Essays: Of Death,* cited in *The Encyclopedia of Religious Quotations,* ed. Frank S. Mead (Old Tappan, N.J.: Fleming H. Revell Company, 1965), p. 98.

[4] Quoted in *The New Dictionary of Thoughts,* Ryan Edwards, comp., and Ralph E. Browns, revision ed.; rev. and enl. by C. N. Catrevas and Jonathan Edwards (New York: Standard Book Co., 1954), p. 345.

[5] William Cowper, "On Invalids," Mead, *op. cit.,* p. 100.

[6] William Wordsworth, "The Excursion," book 4, in *The Complete Works of Wordsworth,* ed. Alice J. George (Boston: Houghton Mifflin Company, 1932), p. 461.

[7] Quoted in Thomas C. Clark and Hazel D. Clark, comps. and eds., *The Golden Book of Immortality* (New York: Association Press, 1954), p. 36.

[8] Quoted in Charles L. Wallis, ed., *Speakers' Illustrations for Special Days* (New York: Abingdon Press, 1956), p. 90.

HOPE ALONG WITH ME, *W. Randall Lolley*

[1] Quoted in Charles L. Wallis, ed., *A Treasury of Sermon Illustrations* (Nashville: Abingdon Press, 1950), p. 59.

[2] *Ibid.,* pp. 165-166.

A TICKET TO WHEREVER IT IS, *William P. Tuck*

[1] Loren Eiseley, from a university address in J. A. Battle and Robert L. Shannon, eds., *The New Idea in Education* (New York: Harper & Row, Publishers, 1968), pp. 46-47.

[2] Eric Marshall and Stuart Hample, comps., *Children's Letters to God* (New York: Essandess Special Editions, a division of Simon & Schuster, Inc., 1966), p. 9.

[3] Dag Hammarskjöld, *Markings* (New York: Alfred A. Knopf, Inc., 1964), p. 213.

[4] Henry James, ed., *The Letters of William James* (Boston: The Atlantic Monthly Press, 1920), vol. 1, p. 129.

[5] Dietrich Bonhoeffer, *Letters and Papers from Prison,* ed. Eberhard Bethge; trans. Reginald H. Fuller (New York: Macmillan Publishing Co., Inc., 1953), p. 14.

[6] Viktor E. Frankl, "The Will to Meaning," in Paul Tournier et al., *Are You Nobody?* (Richmond: John Knox Press, 1966), pp. 26-27.

[7] Albert Schweitzer, *Out of My Life and Thought,* trans. C. T. Compion (New York: Holt, Rinehart and Winston, Inc., 1961), p. 85.

[8] Gerald Kennedy, comp. *A Reader's Notebook* (New York: Harper & Row, Publishers, 1953), p. 311.